Undaunted Heart

UNDAUNTED
HEART

The True Story of a Southern Belle
&
a Yankee General

Suzy Barile

eno
publishers

Eno Publishers
P.O. Box 158
Hillsborough, North Carolina 27278
www.enopublishers.org

Design and typesetting by Dave Wofford
of Horse & Buggy Press in Durham, North Carolina.

ISBN-13: 978-0-9820771-1-5
ISBN-10: 0-9820771-1-4
Library of Congress Control Number: 2009927182

Distributed to the book trade by John F. Blair Publisher, 800-222-9796

Printed in the United States
10 9 8 7 6 5 4 3 2

To my mother, Eleanor Hope Newell Maynard (1927–1991),
a journalist who dreamed of one day telling Ella's story

Table of Contents

Preface   xiii

CHAPTER 1   A Wooing Begins   1

CHAPTER 2   Poetry & Prejudice   19

CHAPTER 3   The Talk & the Curse of the Town   33

CHAPTER 4   A General Is Born   49

CHAPTER 5   Wedding Vows   61

CHAPTER 6   The Wide-Awake Life   71

CHAPTER 7   Anne   81

CHAPTER 8   Life on Prospect Terrace   89

CHAPTER 9   My Desolate Home   101

CHAPTER 10   Moving On   115

CHAPTER 11   Ella   131

CHAPTER 12   Legacies   141

CHAPTER 13   The General   155

Notes   169

Family Tree   207

Bibliography & References   211

Index   223

Acknowledgments   235

Biography   237

Preface

WHEN I WAS A LITTLE GIRL, my granny would hold out her hands, point to her rings, and say to my sister and me, "Ellie, when you grow up, this ring will be yours. Suzy, when you grow up, this ring will be yours." We'd hug her and wonder how long it would be before we were grown!

The ring that became mine was Granny's wedding ring. The one promised my sister had once been the wedding ring of Eleanor (Ella) Hope Swain Atkins.

My sister and I are the descendants of two North Carolina governors. But our most famous ancestor is probably Ella Swain. Many have heard her story. The daughter of state governor and University of North Carolina President David Lowry Swain, Ella did the unthinkable: She married a Yankee general at the close of the Civil War. A North-South marriage at that time flew in "the face of, in the very teeth of all this bitterness and woeful humiliation," explained Chapel Hill's Civil War-era chronicler Cornelia Phillips Spencer.

The meeting, courtship, and marriage of Ella Swain and Union General Smith Dykins Atkins gave North Carolinians a lot to talk about for generations. Their story even made its way into state history books. But over time, the facts of Ella and the general's love story gave way to colorful legend.

In 1949, my mother, Eleanor Hope ("Wuff") Newell—great-granddaughter of Ella and the general—wrote, "Few people have ever heard the real ending. For them, the story simply closes with . . . [her] marrying a Yankee general and with the villagers completely disgusted with her and her entire family."

Always overlooked, she maintained, was the story's happy ending.

Nearly a century and a half after Ella and the general met, I found a cardboard folder in my mother's attic that contained Ella's letters to her parents. The correspondence revealed a love that transcended the bitterness of war and scandal.

After reading Ella's words, I knew I had to tell their story.

CHAPTER I

A Wooing Begins

EASTER SUNDAY 1865 in Chapel Hill was unlike any other. Despite the brilliant spring day, villagers were anxious. The news was grim: Richmond, the capital of the Confederacy, had fallen; so too had Raleigh. Rumors of General Robert E. Lee's surrender had just been confirmed.

The small Southern town that was home to the University of North Carolina, the nation's oldest state university, braced itself as the Union army approached. About mid-day, a paroled Confederate prisoner arrived, wrote local merchant Charles B. Mallett to his soldier-son, alerting everyone to a brigade moving "at full force on the town road, which of course produced great excitement."

Intensifying fears were reports that the brigade was under the command of the notorious General Judson Kilpatrick, nicknamed "Kill-Cavalry" by his own men. He was rumored to have once boasted that his route through the South would be marked by "chimney stacks without houses."

Everyone had thought Chapel Hill would never be captured. The war that had raged through much of the South for four years had never come close enough for town residents to worry about their safety, much less that of the university. When Union General William T. Sherman's troops left Savannah and marched north toward the Carolinas in early 1865, Raleigh resident Kemp Plummer Battle sent "a silver coffee-pot and other silver articles for safekeeping" to his parents, Judge and Mrs. W.H. Battle, in Chapel Hill.

Now nothing seemed safe.

Chapel Hillians prepared for the worst. Judge Battle buried five packages of money, jewelry, and a silver service (possibly the same one his son had sent earlier) in the woods near his home. Professor Charles Phillips and his family hid their silver in a horseradish bed and their watches in the university's telescope, assuming Sherman's cavalry would have no interest in stargazing. Out of concern for the university and its property, library books and other valuable papers were moved to Old East, the students' dormitory, and President David Lowry Swain's home.

"Between sundown and dark some forty or fifty [Union soldiers] . . . came dashing into the village," wrote Charles Mallett. They assured citizens that the town and university would be protected and saved from plundering. They also informed town leaders that Confederate General Joseph E. Johnston would surrender to Sherman the very next day at Durham Station—only eight miles away. The soldiers then retreated.

The next morning, Monday, April 17, "four thousand cavalry entered about eight a.m. and we were captured," wrote Cornelia Phillips Spencer, who chronicled daily events in Chapel Hill during and after the war:

> That was surely a day to be remembered by us all. For the first time in four years we saw the old flag—the "Stars and Stripes," in whose defense we would once have been willing to die, but which certainly excited very little enthusiasm now. Never before had we realized how entirely our hearts had

been turned away from what was once our whole country, till we felt the bitterness aroused by the sight of that flag shaking out its red and white folds over us. . . . The utmost quiet and order prevailed [in Chapel Hill].

Though some estimated the occupying force numbered only four to five hundred, the men in blue overwhelmed the residents and their resources. Quartered at the university and in every home, they required food and care for themselves and their horses.

The soldiers were a tired bunch. They included infantry from Ohio and Michigan, and the Ninety-second Illinois Volunteers, a mounted cavalry. The brigade had been with Sherman when he captured Raleigh on April 13, and it was given orders to march on to Chapel Hill.

Along the way, near Morrisville Station, the soldiers encountered an enemy band led by Confederate Major General Joseph Wheeler. A four-mile chase ensued before the brigade received orders to halt, allowing the Confederates to get away. For the next two days, the Union soldiers endured torrential rain that washed out bridges and forced them to camp and forage off the land along New Hope Creek.

Meanwhile, Wheeler's troops retreated to Chapel Hill, arriving on Good Friday to heroes' welcomes, wrote Mrs. Spencer, as prolific a writer then as she now is controversial for her unflinching Confederate sympathies. The whole town turned out to greet them: "The streets were lined with girls, offering smiles, food, and flowers. It gives me a cheering sensation to see so many gallant fellows—eager to fight and hopeful."

Among the young women welcoming them was twenty-two-year-old Ella Swain, youngest daughter of university President Swain and his wife, Eleanor. The Swains (including Ella, her older sister, Anne, and brother, Richard) were Chapel Hill's most prominent family, occupying the President's House, diagonally across tree-lined Franklin Street from Mrs. Spencer's home. The Swains entertained students, faculty, and noted visitors on the wide porch of their two-story wooden residence. Graceful, tall windows lined the front of the house, giving the Swains an unobstructed view of the comings and goings of townspeople—and of armies.

For the Swains and all their neighbors, the war hit close to home. Though Chapel Hill had been, in Mrs. Swain's words, "remote from the scenes of war," men young and old from the university and town eagerly signed up to fight.

At the start of the war, then-freshman Lavender R. Ray of Georgia described "great excitement here" in an April 1861 letter to his sister:

> Everybody talks, thinks, and dreams of war. The students are leaving daily. The village military departed yesterday, accompanied by twelve or fifteen students who joined them as privates. There is another company being formed here composed mostly of students. They wish to go to Washington City. I desire very much to join them and will do so, if Pa and Ma are willing. I shall await their answer with impatience, hoping it will be affirmative.

Students were not the only ones to join. UNC faculty and families also volunteered. Professor William J. Martin, who taught chemistry, mineralogy, and geology, raised a company of soldiers. Fred and Will Fetter, sons of Greek professor Manuel Fetter, fought at Bethel.

Ella's own brother, twenty-four-year-old Richard (nicknamed Bunkey), joined the Confederate army in 1862, leaving his medical practice in Weldon, North Carolina. For months, while he served as an assistant surgeon, the Swains had not heard from him. This

Portrait of Bunkey and Ella Swain (circa 1850).

was particularly unsettling for Ella, who was close to Bunkey, their fondness captured by a portrait that hung in the Swain home of the two seated side-by-side, a kitten in Ella's arms.

Bunkey was one of the lucky ones—he came home. But many soldiers did not. Judge Battle lost two sons: Junius, twenty-one, died early in the war, while his twenty-year-old brother, Wesley Lewis, died at Gettysburg. Like the Battles, Charles Mallett lost two sons: Richardson, who had graduated from UNC in 1862, was killed at Gettysburg, and Edward died at Bentonville and was survived by a seriously ill wife and four young children.

Kemp Battle, a brother to two fallen soldiers and later president of UNC, wrote that when a loved one was lost, the entire village grieved, for the inhabitants were so few, that the students were known to all, either personally or by reputation.

Not only had Chapel Hillians sacrificed many men to the Confederate cause, but life at home had been full of hardship. Even though it had been spared the carnage and destruction of battle, the town was far from the railroad and telegraph wires, which only "added to the nervous anxieties as to happenings at the front, and almost unsettled reason," explained Battle. "Imagination not corrected by facts, fed itself with fancied triumphs or dismal forebodings."

Residents, like many others throughout the Confederacy, had endured shortages of food and necessities, and suffered inflated prices for what little there was to buy. By spring 1865, a barrel of flour cost $1,000, according to J.B. Jones, a clerk in the Confederate War Department in Richmond. People survived, Mrs. Spencer wrote, "on corn-bread, sorghum, and peas. . . . Children went barefoot through the winter, and ladies made their own shoes, and wove their own homespuns. . . . Curtains were cut up into blankets."

The women who remained behind united with others in supporting the Confederacy both materially, by gathering clothing, food, and medicine, and spiritually, by praying and fasting for peace. Ella, who was eighteen when the war began, helped collect much-needed supplies, including shoes and knitted items, for members of the Fourth Texas Regiment after learning its soldiers were going barefooted. Mrs. Spencer described the undertaking as "a token to them of our love and sympathy."

In spite of the war's devastating toll, the University of North Carolina had managed to keep its doors open, even with a meager enrollment of fewer than twenty students at war's end. President Swain, who served three terms as governor of North Carolina, had led his alma mater for thirty years.

An early and ardent opponent of secession, Swain initially had advised students and faculty to keep politics out of the classroom; but when the Confederacy was formed, he remained true to his home state and supported the cause.

* * * * *

WHEN WHEELER'S MEN streamed into Chapel Hill that Friday afternoon after skirmishing with the Union troops, people put aside the burdens of war and offered the soldiers their best. Most residents had "not a chair but a split-bottom in the house, not a fork but a two-pronged iron, not six tumblers, nor a single set of table ware of any sort, not a carpet or a curtain or a napkin, not a castor, not a single article of luxury in the house—not even a common rocking chair," Mrs. Spencer noted. Yet all were "generally—always I may say—heartily welcomed."

Everyone knew the celebration would be short-lived: With the Union army nearing, any Confederate soldier found in Chapel Hill when they arrived would become a prisoner of war.

Surrender was bitter, but the prospect of peace after years of war provided some consolation. Raleigh resident Emma White wrote to her nieces Ella and Anne Swain in Chapel Hill:

> I pray that our Heavenly Father may look with pity and compassion on us, and . . . illuminate every part of our Southern Confederacy. . . . Every few days we hear a Yankee cavalry of immense force is about to leave Newbern to make a raid to this place & that deters us. We feel that we ought not to think of leaving home during such times of excitement.

No one understood the consequences of the surrender better than did President Swain, who three days earlier—accompanied by another former North Carolina governor, William A. Graham—had traveled to Raleigh to meet with General Sherman to negotiate the state's surrender.

Their mission on behalf of North Carolina Governor Zebulon B. Vance was dangerous. However, both men felt it their duty to complete the task. Several years later, President Swain described that assignment:

> It was my lot on the morning of the 13th of April, 1865, as the friend and representative of Gov. Vance, to find, on approaching the Southern front of the Capitol, the doors and windows closed, and a deeper, more dreadful silence shrouding the city.

At the Capitol, he was met by "a negro servant, who waited on the executive department, the only human being who had dared venture beyond his door."

> He delivered me the keys and assisted me in opening the doors and windows of the executive office, and I took my station at the entrance, with a safe conduct from Gen. Sherman in my hand, prepared to surrender the Capitol at the demand of his approaching forces.
>
> At that moment a band of marauders, stragglers from Wheeler's retiring cavalry, dismounted at the head of First Street, and began to sack the stores directly contiguous to and south of Dr. [Fabius] Haywood's residence. I apprised them immediately, that Sherman's army was just at hand, that any show of resistance might result in the destruction of the city, and urged them to follow their retreating comrades.

A citizen, the first I saw beyond his threshold that morning, came up at the moment and united his remonstrance's to mine, but all in vain, until I perceived and announced that the head of [General] Kilpatrick's column was in sight. In a moment, every member of the band, with the exception of their chivalric leader, was in the saddle and his horse spurred to his utmost speed. He drew his bridle rein, halted in the centre of the street, and discharged his revolver until his stock of ammunition was expended in the direction, but not in carrying distance of his foe, when he too fled, but attempted to run the gauntlet in vain. His life was the forfeit at a very brief interval.

About 3 o'clock in the evening, in company with Gov. Graham, who had risked life and reputation on behalf of this community to an extent, of which those who derived the advantage are little aware, I delivered the keys of the State House to Gen. Sherman, at the gubernatorial mansion, then his headquarters, and received his assurance that the Capitol and city should be protected, and the rights of private property duly regarded.

Back home two days later, President Swain watched as Wheeler and his troops came and went. Knowing the Union army would soon arrive, Wheeler's men didn't stay long. By early afternoon on Easter Sunday, they headed west. "Once more, and for the last time," Mrs. Spencer wrote, "we saw the gallant sight of our gray-clad Confederate soldiers, and waved our last farewell to our army. . . . We sat in our pleasant piazzas, and awaited events with a quiet resignation."

What lay ahead was "the most remarkable three weeks in the history of Chapel Hill. . . . We could rely on nothing we heard." Residents "talked and speculated, while the very peace and profound quiet of the place sustained and soothed our minds."

* * * * *

HOW WOULD THE TOWN that days before had celebrated Wheeler's Confederate soldiers now receive the Yankees? Early Easter evening, a committee of town leaders met Captain J.M. Schermerhorn of the Ninety-second Illinois on Raleigh Road at the edge of Chapel Hill. Carrying a white handkerchief tied to a pole, the committee included President Swain, Judge Battle, and Wilson Swain, the son of the Swains' slave, Rosa Burgess.

By birth, wrote Kemp Battle, Wilson Swain was considered to be a slave and was given the last name of his owner. But he had been raised by the Swains as a playmate for their son, Bunkey, and had been educated alongside him.

Captain Schermerhorn announced that Union troops, camped nearby, were advancing and intended to take Chapel Hill. President Swain informed him that he personally had been assured by General Sherman when they had met in Raleigh that no harm would come to the campus or town. Schermerhorn acknowledged that those were his orders. Kemp Battle later mused that Wilson Swain's presence in particular made a positive impression on the Union officer. Even so, before rejoining his company, the captain searched the streets for enemy soldiers.

It was a peaceful surrender the next morning when the soldiers, led by General Smith Dykins Atkins of the Ninety-second Illinois, marched into the village. He would later remember Chapel Hill as "one of the prettiest, most lovely spots found in all the campaigning of the 92nd during its three years service."

Brigade commander for the feared General Kilpatrick, Smith Atkins seemed to have none of his commanding officer's bluster or aggressiveness, much to the relief of townspeople. Even he had once described Kilpatrick as being "as quick-witted as he was impatient."

General Atkins immediately called on the town's leading official, President Swain, who greeted him graciously. As they talked, the two men, who had been on opposite sides of a long, hard-fought war, found they had much in common: Both had grown up in frontier towns; both were lawyers and politicians; both loved history.

Raised on a farm outside Freeport, Illinois, Atkins attended college, then read for the law and passed the bar exam at age twenty. The young general's story may have sounded familiar to President Swain, whose boyhood was spent in the mountains of western North Carolina. Swain left there at age twenty-one, also to prepare for the bar, at the University of North Carolina and in Raleigh. He returned home in 1823 to practice law; a year later he was elected to the state legislature, before being named a circuit judge. David Swain was then elected by the legislature to be governor of North Carolina in the 1830s.

Smith Atkins started practicing law in Freeport in 1856. Four years later, after campaigning for Abraham Lincoln and making a number of well-received speeches, he was elected to a four-year term as state's attorney for the state judicial circuit, serving his home county of Stephenson, and two nearby counties.

He had grown up hearing family war stories. His grandfather, David H. Atkins, was a soldier during the Revolutionary War, serving under Colonel Levi Pawling and Captain Frederick Schoonmaker with the Third Regiment Ulster County (New York) Militia. His father, Adna Stanly Atkins, was traveling in England in 1812 when he received news of impending war and quickly returned to join the United States army. Both men inspired Smith Atkins and his brothers to enlist.

At age twenty-five, he first marched off to war in what the local paper called "a stirring day in Freeport. Three thousand citizens of the city went out to cheer them on. . . ." Now, four years later, Atkins was a general, sitting in the home of former North Carolina governor David Swain.

Out of deference to his host, General Atkins most likely didn't talk about his reasons for joining the Union army: To defend his country against what he believed was the treason of secession and to end slavery, which he abhorred.

In 1860, Smith Atkins had spoken against the U.S. Supreme Court's *Dred Scott* decision, an 1857 ruling challenging the constitutionality of congressional anti-slavery efforts in the federal territories:

> If they [the South] will not listen to the voice of reason, we
> must exchange our lamps for Sharpe's rifles, and to what
> we have already said, we must add the eloquent language of
> gunpowder, & the inexorable convincing argument of lead. . . .
> I am ready to cry out against human bondage in any & every
> form. I hate slavery.

On the April morning President Swain and General Atkins met, newly freed slaves were at work in the Swain residence. Like many prominent Southern families, the Swains had been slave owners. President Swain listed forty slaves in his 1855 ledger. It's doubtful his household included that number by the end of the Civil War. He, in fact, wrote former Governor William Graham in May 1865, "Four of my men ran off . . . three have returned, but only one is on my premises." He added that though the women and children "wish to remain, I cannot afford to keep them, and am loathe to drive them away."

The Swains referred to their slaves as servants. Scattered throughout the family's correspondence and in their Bible were references to their *colored friends.* Similarly, in records at Chapel of the Cross, the town's Episcopal church, the names, baptisms, marriages, and funerals of both white and black members were listed on the same pages, differentiated by the words *servant of* or *belonging to* with the owner's name. The word *colored* was written in parenthesis.

Given the situation, it's likely the two men discussed the safer subject of the history of the American Revolution, which both had studied. Little did they know that their shared interest would lead to a personal revolution that would transform their lives. It all began when President Swain asked someone to bring him a history book to show the general.

* * * * *

IMAGINE THIS: The dogwood trees and wisteria blossom along the streets of Chapel Hill, as Atkins's men, horses, and accoutrements of battle spread throughout town, and residents look on in sorrow and resignation, realizing the war has been lost. Meanwhile, in the parlor of the Swain house, two leaders chat amiably while servants and family members eavesdrop in the hallway.

Offering to show his guest a map of Lord Cornwallis's route through North Carolina during the Revolutionary War, President Swain calls for someone to bring him the book containing the map.

His daughter Ella—a faithful supporter of the Confederacy, but no less curious to see this Yankee—responds. As her neighbor Mrs. Spencer would later recall, she "threw up her head and marched in with great display of hauteur." When she hands her father the book, he has no choice but to introduce her to the Yankee general.

* * * * *

S EVERAL VERSIONS OF ELLA'S INTRODUCTION to the general have been woven into Chapel Hill lore. Colonel W.D. Hamilton with the Ninth Ohio Cavalry told of meeting "a number of young people of the town . . . one of the most attractive . . . Miss Ella was as brilliant and original as she was elegant and attractive."

She had a quick wit, telling Hamilton, "Well, you Yankees have got here at last. We have been looking for you for some time, and have a curiosity to know what you are going to do with us." Pointing out that the soldiers had "destroyed our country and our means of support; you have burned our fences and many of our homes and factories; you have disorganized and robbed us of our labor; you have killed or disabled our young men, at least the best of them, but the women are all here."

Then she asked, "What are you going to do with us?"

Taken aback by her "strangely bright face as she presented this formidable indictment," Hamilton responded that the Yankees might follow the ancient Fabians' custom—"after they had overrun a neighboring province and killed the men, began the reconstruction of the country by marrying the women."

Ella remained cool. "We are at your mercy; but I suppose you will let us have something to say about that."

What Hamilton had in mind was introducing her to "a very gallant friend" with "personal energy, high character, and ability," and a bachelor who "always expected to remain one."

The next evening he did just that, although Atkins insisted he did not "want to make any social calls" before finally consenting. Hamilton recalled:

I gave my attention to the ladies of the previous evening, while the General devoted himself to Miss Swain. About 10 o'clock I suggested that it was time to go to camp. He replied that it was not late.

Some time afterward I repeated the suggestion. He responded, "yes, in a few minutes."

After another interval I said if we remained much longer we would have trouble, as I had not the countersign. He replied that he had it.

When Hamilton went looking for Atkins the next afternoon, he found him at the Swains "on some matter of business. It was the old, old story. A feathered arrow from the ancient bow had pierced the heart the modern bullet had failed to reach."

* * * * *

A DIFFERENT STORY about their introduction came from a member of the Illinois State Historical Society who claimed that Ella and the general met when

it became his [Atkins's] duty, as a matter of form, to arrest the president of the State University . . . David L. Swain, one of North Carolina's distinguished sons who had been the governor of the state.

Little did young Colonel Atkins . . . expect that he was going to such a complete surrender to a southern victor.

With southern courtesy, Governor Swain invited his captor to his home. The family tradition is that the youngest daughter, Miss Eleanor [Ella], stated to her father that she was not going to sit at the same table with that young Yankee. However, as the Governor intimated that such conduct would not be polite, she consented to sit at the table, but declared that she would not say one word to him.

Upon seeing her, Atkins "decided that there should be a union of the states at once, so far as he was concerned, and with his usual firm determination he succeeded in securing the young lady's consent to marry him, before he went away that night."

Still another version of the introduction was told by historian Charles Lee Smith, who described Sherman's order that the University of North Carolina "be protected from pillage and destruction" as "done very effectually. General Atkins, while visiting President Swain on official business, accidentally saw his daughter; he afterwards sought her acquaintance, addressed her, and was accepted."

Regardless of which telling is true, no one disputes Mrs. Spencer's vivid remembrance: Atkins and Ella "'changed eyes' at first sight and a wooing followed."

CHAPTER 2

Poetry & Prejudice

K ILPATRICK'S BRIGADE made itself at home. Within days of Ella and General Atkins's introduction, the Union soldiers and cavalry silver cornet band were serenading the village. Atkins later would recall many occasions during the war when his soldiers lifted their voices in song. In Raleigh they once had asked permission "to sing to several young ladies standing in front of a school. Not until they noticed the members of their audience making motions with their hands did the singers realize the girls were deaf, and the school was the State School for the Deaf."

Atkins wrote a third-person account of an evening in Chapel Hill when the serenading—a popular pastime—was directed at him:

> On the evening of the twenty-second . . . the Ninety-Second boys, with the band, proceeded to the head-quarters of General Atkins to serenade him; and, finding him absent, they proceeded to the residence of ex-Governor Swain, where the General was visiting, and serenaded him there. . . . They called on the General for a speech, when he appeared upon the front porch . . . and said: "Soldiers, I am making a speech

to a young lady here tonight, and I have no eloquance [*sic*] to waste—she requires it all. The war, as I told you it would, at Mount Olive, has played out, and in less than the ninety days I then named. I think speech-making has played out also, except to the young ladies. You must go to your quarters."

Those words were "the most unpopular" ever, Atkins wrote years later in the *Ninety-Second Illinois Volunteers*, for "never before, when serenaded by the men of the Ninety-Second—and it had often happened—had he failed to appreciate the compliment, and had always responded cheerfully to their calls for a speech." He was too infatuated with Miss Ella to offer any words of wisdom to his troops, explaining, "The General was cross in those days to every one, except the girl he was making love to."

Even though serenading typically was viewed as an expression of gratitude, town residents were none too pleased. They resented anything and everything associated with their Yankee captors.

The general hardly noticed. He was busy courting Ella and writing poetry. On April 19, just two days after they met, Atkins gave her an acrostic in which he began each line with the letters in her name:

M y pen in poetry never deals,

I n woman's praise, and such like things;

S ometimes it tells what my heart feels,

S ometimes proclaims what my heart sings.

E ver of "Hope" my heart hath sung:

L owly and soft as a vesper song,

L ifting the shadows around me flung,

A s the dawn have bourn my life along.

"H ope" in the song is ever bright–

O f "Hope" my heart is singing gladly–

P luck from the song "Hope's" beautiful light–

E ver the song would be murmured sadly.

S ing my heart does, a wayward song,

W hether of love I can hardly tell–

A low sweet music murmurs along.

I n mind, strange accents like the swell

N ear a bachelor's bower of a marriage bell.

After presenting it to her, Atkins read the poem to his friend Captain D.L. Cockley, telling him that Ella had not liked the wording and demanded he change it not once, but twice: "Miss Ella was very hard to please, and did not like the 'accroustic' [*sic*] at all. She made very bitter complaint of the second line in the last verse, so I changed it to read 'Which is of love, if I can tell.'"

Ella still was not satisfied, according to General Atkins:

"The little minx would not be pleased," [Atkins] explained,
"until I changed it again ('three times and out' you know) and
made it read: 'Which is of love, I know full well.' Then the
little tantalizer kissed me and professed herself satisfied."

With great pleasure, Ella promptly showed the poem to Mrs. Spencer, describing the change she had insisted upon ("An acrostic not good either but his first sentiment as well as song") and showing her Atkins's photograph.

Though Atkins recalled changing the second line of the last verse right away, Ella told Mrs. Spencer he changed it "in a note to me the day he left CH ('Which is of love I now can tell'). . . . You see from this it was a gradual affair," Ella explained, before admitting, "Ellie is caught at last in her own net."

She coyly returned Atkins's attentions, asking him to sign her autograph book, a privilege reserved for friends to write sentiments and poems. He obliged with *Very Truly Yours, Smith D. Atkins Freeport, Illinois,* adding a flourish to the date *April 22, 1865.*

As was evident from other autographers, Ella was very attractive. Edward A.P. Nicholson of Halifax County opined, *Oh thou! Whose blameless life combined soft female charms and grace combined. . . . May prosperity attend thee through life.* T. Stuart Armistead of Plymouth pleaded, *Forget me not but let my memory linger.* Frederick R. Bryan of Raleigh declared, *May life be as a summer's day to thee.*

* * * * *

NOT EVERYONE IN CHAPEL HILL approved of the way in which President Swain was handling the Union occupation. He kept the university open, though some thought that classes should have been cancelled, considering the situation. Charles Mallett wrote to his son:

> I feel provoked to hear the college bell sounding as though the college was in full blast—a miserable set—not one true man among them and they desire to hand it down in history that the dear Yankees, did not interfere with the regular exercise of the college—when in truth there were not five students here when Wheeler left us.

Chapel Hillians were scandalized by the conduct of the young women, particularly that of Ella Swain. Although Mallett described Atkins as "a Gentleman and a Lawyer," he criticized the young women who were flirting with the Yankees:

> I learn that Misses Fetters are walking the streets with them, and Miss Ella Swain sent to Carrie [Mallett's grand-daughter] to borrow her side saddle to ride out with some officer—Several other Ladies—or I would rather call them women—have been riding out with them. . . . My guard also informs me (and he believes it) that his captain is to be married before they leave to Miss [Susan] Fetter—certainly those girls with Beck Ryan and Ella Swain have lain themselves open to much scandal.

One of the few existing photographs of Ella Swain, taken sometime between 1856 and 1858.

Much to her family's relief, Miss Fetter did not marry the Union soldier.

Within the Swain household, however, tension was mounting. Even though Ella and Atkins were wooing, and Atkins and David Swain had become fast friends, Mrs. Swain had no interest in friendship with the general or anyone in the Union army, "so great was her hate for the Yankees," wrote her great-great-granddaughter "Wuff" Newell years later.

When her husband invited Atkins to dinner, Mrs. Swain refused to join them at the table, a form of protest she surprisingly would never give up. She wrote her friend Selina Wheat, "We will never give up the strife until exterminated or freed and restored to a peaceful security and our own independence."

Her feelings were shared by many. Southern women, wrote historian Marilyn Meyer Culpepper, "suffered most from displacement, pillaging, and harassment" with battles "fought at their doorstep. . . . Their hatred of the North had become an obsession and any thought of reconciliation was anathema."

Their bitterness was further exacerbated by what Mrs. Swain's cousin Mary Gatlin described as the "deplorable condition" in which many Southerners were forced to live.

The village of Chapel Hill had paid a particularly high price, Mrs. Spencer lamented:

> Not a village in the South gave more freely of its best blood
> in the war, not one suffered more severely in proportion to
> its population. Thirty-five of our young men died in the
> service. Some of them left wives and little ones; some were
> the only support and blessing of aged parents; all were, with
> very few exceptions, the very flower of our families, and
> were representatives of every walk and condition of life.

Colonel Smith D. Atkins of the Ninety-second
Illinois Volunteers (circa 1862).

The dramatic decline in enrollment at the university had thrown
"many of our citizens out of employment, and the privations endured
here tell as sad a story as can be met with anywhere," Mrs. Spencer
wrote. Fall semester 1864 at UNC began with fewer than fifty students.
By April 1865, only a handful of local students remained. Low enrollment meant little revenue.

President Swain had struggled to keep the university's doors open
throughout the war. He frequently traveled to Raleigh on university
business, staying with his wife's sisters, Emma and Susan White at
White Hall, the family home. After one visit, Emma wrote Eleanor
that David's demeanor had been "very low spirited—what is the cause
I know not. It may be the state of the country or his not feeling well or
perhaps both together that makes him so sad."

Conditions at the university and in the town weighed heavily on President Swain. By the time the Union soldiers arrived in Chapel Hill, "some families were left, first, without a morsel of food," General Atkins observed in *Ninety-Second Illinois Volunteers,* "and, again, with many mouths, colored and white, to provide for, without an animal to make a crop of corn with, the coming season."

Clearly "there was no help for it," he wrote. "'Such is war,' and there is no use in attempting to refine it. Useless cruelty in war, and to the defenseless inhabitants of a country occupied by an army, is, of course, indefensible; but 'war is cruelty,' and the cruelty that ensued from an army subsisting upon the country was not useless. . . . Wheeler's cavalry had 'lived upon the country'. . . and there was little left to live upon."

So extreme was the deprivation of town residents that Swain wrote to General Sherman, asking that the soldiers be more mindful of the needs of their hosts:

> Many worthy families have been stripped by his soldiers of the necessary means of subsistence. A Baptist clergyman— a most estimable, quiet, and charitable citizen, and the most extensive farmer within a circle of three miles—is almost entirely destitute of provision for man and beast; and with a family of more than fifty persons, white and colored, has not a single horse or mule. . . . Mr. Purefoy . . . my near neighbor for about thirty years . . . is not merely without the present means of subsistence, but unless his horses and mules are restored or replaced, can make no provision for the future. The delay of a few days even may render it impossible to plant corn in proper time.

As her father tried to improve Chapel Hillians' living conditions, and her mother refused to join a Union visitor at the dinner table, Ella seemed oblivious. The young woman who so recently had scorned the Yankees was falling in love with one.

She wrote Mrs. Spencer:

> As to myself, but one voice can prevent this "affair," & that is higher than man. No indeed, I have all I desire in most noble heart & mind entrusted to my keeping. I trust you did not think me so wanting in true refinement that I would have been willing to allow this exhibition?
>
> I had nothing to hide when the Yankees came except myself. I had no fear of being stolen, but see the result.

* * * * *

TWO WEEKS AFTER ELLA SWAIN and General Atkins met, the Ninety-second Illinois received orders to muster out. It was the third time in a week that orders had come, only to be rescinded. First, on April 24, when terms of General Johnston's surrender were not accepted, the soldiers had been advised to prepare to resume hostilities; but they never left. Two days later they were instructed to be ready to march at daylight. Again, they remained in place. But on April 29, General Kilpatrick arrived in Chapel Hill to inspect the brigade, a sure sign the soldiers would be leaving soon.

For Ella, it was unsettling to know General Atkins would leave but not to know when.

Finally on May 3—nearly three years to the day since the Ninety-second had left Freeport—the soldiers withdrew from Chapel Hill for Hillsborough, twelve miles away. Atkins recalled that along the way they frequently met Confederate soldiers:

[Our] late enemies, enemies no longer, filled the road, and together they marched. . . . The Confederate soldiers were somewhat downcast and dispirited, but the Ninety-Second men, who had frequently met them in battle, had no jibes for them; they had learned, on many a hard-fought field, how brave the Confederate soldiers under Wheeler and Hampton were; they respected their bravery; indeed, gray-coat and blue-coat, mingling together in their march that day through Hillsboro, were friends, enemies no longer, but friends and equals, all citizens of the Republic saved.

They then marched on to Greensboro, Lexington, Salisbury, and finally Concord—which Atkins described as "a stylish camp" in a grove of pine trees. But the men found little to do there but wonder when they would be sent home—"all wished to return at once to those peaceful pursuits they had reluctantly left when they volunteered to help maintain the life of the nation."

Ready as they were to be discharged, the Ninety-second was held back by General Kilpatrick in case he needed a mounted cavalry moved quickly into place. Consequently, on May 21, when the U.S. War Department announced that all foot soldiers of the infantry regiments be mustered out immediately, it did not include the Ninety-second.

During the weeks of waiting, Smith Atkins returned briefly to Chapel Hill to see Ella. Mrs. Spencer recorded the following in her diary:

Have just seen Ellie Swain dressed and waiting for General Atkins who drove into town a few moments ago. Dressed in a lavender [dress] and pink ribbons . . . pink oleander blossom on her bosom. So bright—so happy! Are there any days more happy in life than such? . . . The brightest and sunniest picture is that of a young woman with love-lighted eyes and throbbing heart prettily and tastefully adorned and waiting to see her lover. I have a great deal of respect for true love and all his belongings.

When General Atkins arrived back in Concord, he found that his troops still had not received word that they could return to Illinois, causing much grumbling and "harsh language." Then on June 21, news came that the war department had released all cavalry. Finally, the Ninety-second could go home.

Back in Chapel Hill, Ella had news of her own: She and General Atkins were engaged.

CHAPTER 3

The Talk & the Curse of the Town

WORD OF ELLA SWAIN'S betrothal to a Yankee was met with disbelief and outrage. President Swain, who had been consumed with his duties to North Carolina, the South, and the university, "was suddenly saddled with an unexpected family problem which immediately became the talk and the curse of the town," wrote historian James Vickers in *Chapel Hill: An Illustrated History*. "Others in Chapel Hill were quick to condemn Ellie's 'collaboration.'"

He could do little about the public's angry response to news of his daughter's engagement to a Yankee general. Swain hardly welcomed the idea. Yes, he had befriended Atkins, presenting him with his copy of *Interesting Revolutionary Incidents* and inscribing it, "Gen. S.D. Atkins, from his friend, D.L. Swain. Chapel Hill. 25 April 1865."

But *Atkins the Union general* becoming *Atkins the son-in-law* had not been what Swain had in mind when he gave him the history book.

President Swain became "deeply concerned and agitated," Mrs. Spencer wrote in her journal. "Suddenly his tenderest affections were touched, and in his own household he was called upon to act in a matter requiring the most delicate and cautious management."

Yet, she wrote, he believed similar marriages would take place throughout the North and South at war's end. In fact, after Ella showed Atkins's acrostic to her father, she told Mrs. Spencer, "He wishes me to tell you this fact: professes to be somewhat 'abused' but I think more amused."

If David Swain was upset by his daughter's announcement, Mrs. Swain was distraught. It was not only her hatred of the North that prevented her from approving the match, but genuine concern for her daughter's happiness.

* * * *

A GENERATION EARLIER, the Swains' own courtship had hardly been a romantic fairy tale. In 1822, David Swain was living in Raleigh's Eagle Hotel while studying law with Judge John Louis Taylor, the first chief justice of the state Supreme Court. At that time, conversation parties were popular. In a letter to his father, David described how fifty or so people would assemble in a private home in the evening "in familiar chat, eating and drinking cake, tea, and ice-creams."

It was at just such a party that he met Eleanor White. She was the daughter of William White, former North Carolina Secretary of State, and granddaughter of Richard Caswell, Revolutionary War hero and North Carolina's first governor.

David Swain came from a well-respected family in Buncombe County in the Blue Ridge Mountains. He was the nephew of Joel Lane, who had donated the land on which Raleigh was built. At twenty-two, David was a successful student and well liked by such leaders as Judge Taylor, Joseph and W.R. Gales of the *Raleigh Register*, and lawyer-politician William Gaston.

A portrait of David L. Swain, president of the University of North Carolina.

When David Swain's father, George, asked Judge Taylor about his son's progress, Taylor responded, "[he is] indefatigable in his studies and is not satisfied with a superficial view of any subject he attempts."

These traits could be attributed to his father, who instilled in his son "the pure and simple habits and tastes," Mrs. Spencer later wrote. The elder Swain was "ambitious for him, and ambitious of the best things. He taught his son to choose good company and to aim high."

In matters of the heart, however, young Swain was less successful. He had fallen for Eleanor White, but his love seemed to be unrequited. Eleanor paid him little notice, though some thought she simply was being demure. "She is undoubtedly the lady of the family, and I respect and esteem her, the more I know her," his friend W.R. Gales wrote. Historian Kemp Battle described Eleanor as "a women of fine intellect but retiring disposition, [who] cared nothing for Society."

After a year of studying with Judge Taylor and months of calling on Eleanor White, David Swain passed the bar exam and returned to Buncombe County to practice law. He also campaigned for his half-brother, James Lowry, who was elected to the state House of Commons, and for his friend Dr. Robert Brank Vance, who won a seat in the U.S. Congress. With his new-found taste for politics, Swain decided to run for the House of Commons in 1824, emphasizing local issues and staying away from national controversy over a one-party, five-candidate race for the U.S. presidency (which John Quincy Adams won). Swain's campaign was successful. He was elected and then re-elected four times.

All the while, he corresponded with Eleanor White, making clear that his feelings for her had not changed:

> Whatever may be the sentiments she entertains with regard
> to me, will I trust excuse the liberty I take in addressing this
> note to her, since should the subject prove disagreeable she

will not find me disposed to trespass on the feelings of a lady to whom of all others I would least willing be the source of pain.

In at least one letter, he proposed marriage. How or if she responded isn't known.

While Swain was in Asheville, his friends kept him informed about Eleanor. Gales reported, "[John S.] Ruffin, [R.B.] Ellis & myself . . . are the only young men who regularly visit [the White home] now . . . we are a standing list. Ellis attaches himself almost exclusively to Gartha [a younger sister] . . . I as usual take care of Susan & the old lady [presumably Mrs. White]. . . . [Nothing] would afford me half the pleasure that the union of yourself and Miss . . . would produce," perhaps playfully omitting Eleanor's name. Gales assured him that Eleanor was interested: "I can see by the manner in which you are enquired after by Whitehall that they regard you in the light of a future son-in-law."

Dr. Vance declared Eleanor's intent as *"bona fide cortia,"* writing that "inquiries about the mountains—Swain—and when he was coming— every look, every gesture, every notion was a confirmation."

Buoyed by their encouragement, David Swain wrote to Eleanor shortly after being elected to his first term in the House of Commons:

> Since I learned to entertain for her the most affectionate regard & it is more than 18 mos. since I ventured to express this sentiment. . . . it would be idle to apologize for not venturing to hope that I may be reguarded [*sic*] in a more favorable light. . . . time and distance have never changed the current of my feelings. . . .

He still elicited no promising notice from her.

When David arrived in Raleigh in the fall of 1825 for the legislature, he called on her again. But on one visit, he discovered her receiving "Mr. Hills," who effectively "foiled the propriety of any attempt on my part to bring about an interview without some assurance that it would not be unpleasant to you."

That was the breaking point.

On January 2, 1826, David Swain wrote Eleanor that Mr. Hills's visit had "placed me in a situation . . . delicate and perplexing, and one from which no honorable means of escape are provided without further understanding on the subject." He assured her that he stood by his earlier promise that he had "no disposition to trespass on your feelings. . . ." More than anything, he wanted them to "perfectly understand each other." Some of her actions toward him incited feelings "so long and ardently desired on my part . . . [actions] connected with an idea, that in and of itself was calculated to dash the cup with bittering."

She was toying with his heart and he wasn't happy.

He knew that "conjugal happiness depends entirely on . . . reciprocity of such feelings, and that without this reciprocity, the most tender of earthly ties, is converted into an interminable and indissoluble chain of misery." David asked that she make her true intentions known. If she did not share his feelings, "I wish to part with her, as an interesting and affectionate friend, and in no other point of view."

This heartfelt outpouring got her attention.

Ten days later, on January 12, David Swain and Eleanor White were married at White Hall.

A portrait of Eleanor White Swain from 1840.

* * * * *

THE NEWLYWEDS PROMPTLY MOVED to Asheville. Upon their arrival, David Swain wrote family friend and state treasurer, John Haywood, that the carriage ride through the Blue Ridge Mountains to their new home was difficult, as they "encountered much more snow and mud than was entirely agreeable, even to a mountaineer. . . . The little lady who accompanied me bore up under the fatigue and difficulties of the way, affording comfortable assurance that she would not be found waning amidst the troubles and trials of a journey of greater extent and no longer."

They settled into a rented two-story home, and David Swain resumed his law practice, riding the circuit as the court moved from county to county. But they were not to live happily ever after in Asheville. Eleanor did not like the harsh winter. When spring arrived, she returned to Raleigh's milder climate, moving back to White Hall with her mother and sisters.

David Swain traveled frequently to Raleigh to attend the legislature and to visit Eleanor. In between trips he wrote her often, expressing concern for her health and circumstances. After winning re-election to the House of Commons in the summer of 1826, he wrote:

> My dear Eleanor, Won by 100 votes—campaign [has] been an arduous one. . . . [I] will visit once I hear from you. . . . Be content and happy and think with pleasure on your affectionate husband.

He longed to be with her: "My anxiety to see you increases every day, and it would require a very important consideration to tempt me to undergo three months longer separation."

To allow him to spend more time with his wife, he decided not to run for another term in 1827. But then he was elected a solicitor for the northeastern part of the state, requiring him to be away from Eleanor even more.

On January 20, 1828, after two years of frequent separation, David Swain resigned. Again he was elected to the House of Commons representing Buncombe County; so for part of the year, the couple was together in Raleigh.

Eleanor Swain returned at least once to live in Asheville. David's widowed father, George, became ill in 1828, and the couple moved there to be near him. While caring for him, their first child, Anne, was born on October 9, 1829. But Anne never knew her grandfather, who died two months later, on Christmas Eve.

The following spring, Eleanor and baby Anne moved back to Raleigh, while David Swain remained in Asheville, practicing law and continuing his public service.

* * * * *

IN ELLA'S MATCH with General Atkins, Eleanor Swain perhaps saw history repeating itself, anticipating for her daughter extended periods of separation from her husband and the need to relocate to an unfamiliar place.

Mrs. Swain saw great promise in her youngest child—and wanted a life for her that did not include marrying a Yankee general! The Swains undoubtedly pinned many of their hopes on Ella. Her sister,

Anne, now in her mid-thirties and still living at home, had suffered from mental disorders, requiring frequent hospitalizations and causing the family worry and anxiety. Ella, in contrast, was lively and had a good disposition.

As a girl, Ella was described by her Aunt Susan as "her Pa's joy." Mrs. Spencer recalled her "clinging round the Gov's [Swain's] neck . . . & as she was at six years old—at ten—at fifteen. How pretty, how bright, & sweet & saucy. . . . I always called her 'a white kitten.' She was ever sweet & most attractive to me."

In a letter to Anne, Mrs. Swain had written that young Ella was "very smart" and "willing to learn" but had limited educational opportunities unless she left home to go away to school. In 1857, at age fourteen, Ella did just that, joining other young women from around the state at Edgeworth Female Seminary in Greensboro. Founded in 1840 by former Governor John Motley Morehead to educate his five daughters, Edgeworth had a "highly trained specialist from Europe in charge of art, music and language departments." It was described as "the pride of the town . . . its campus, with shrubbery, rose bowers and many shade trees." There, Ella enjoyed painting, encouraged by Principal Richard Sterling, who taught her how to stretch canvas over a frame.

Ella excelled as a student. Mrs. Swain wrote Anne in 1857:

> Ella keeps very well and is highly pleased with school. I think she is improving rapidly in letter writing. Her style, the writing, spelling too . . . show, that she has learned to think and to work much faster than I could have calculated.
>
> She says she will get the first mark for good behavior in her report next month.

About this time, Ella became serious about religion, which pleased her parents. Mrs. Swain wrote her friend Selina Wheat after Ella professed her faith at a revival at Edgeworth: "I feel so thankful; that she has given herself so early in life to the service of the Lord. . . ."

After leaving Edgeworth, Ella enrolled as a boarding student at Saint Mary's, an Episcopal girls' school in Raleigh, in the early 1860s. Saint Mary's offered young women "a thorough and elegant education, equal to the best that can be obtained in the City of New York, or in any northern school," explained headmaster Reverend Aldert Smedes, who believed in the transformation of "society gradually through the influence of educated Christian women."

He was ahead of his time. Educating young women was still controversial. Even UNC Professor William Hooper thought some schools over-educated women. In an 1832 report to the North Carolina Institute of Education, he insisted, "the young lady, by the time she reaches her teens, is in danger of thinking herself grammarian, geographer, astronomer, chemist, botanist, painter and whatnot."

Rev. Smedes, on the other hand, believed Northern women were better educated; they could converse intelligently with their husbands; and they were better prepared to "provide a good home for their husband and children."

He envisioned more for Southern, churched women.

So, it seems, did Mrs. Swain.

Yet over her parents' objections, Ella Swain remained steadfast in her determination to marry General Atkins.

* * * * *

ELLA WROTE TO MRS. SPENCER, "As to what 'people' say, Pa's great failing is to care too much. . . ." She was irritated that her father had shown Atkins's letters to Mrs. Spencer:

> I never was more surprised, provoked & distressed in my life, than when I found, by accident, this evening, that Pa had been showing letters (to me) of all things on earth the most sacred.
>
> Letters written for my eye alone; & only trusted to my Father as an act of duty; without the least thought that any other than himself should read them.
>
> [He] seeks rather than avoid the opinion & advice of the world. It was enough to have exposed the first letter, but past comprehension, the second. He was guided by what he considered best for me, but very much against my wishes. . . . It takes from the letters their true value to have them reduced to matter of fact, as much as to expose to the world's eye, "the hidden treasures of the heart."

She objected to the idea that her romance would be played out in public. "The world may scorn me if it will / I care but little for its scoffing," she declared, then thanked Mrs. Spencer for "your kind 'endorsement'" and expressed "hope this secret may be kept."

But word of the engagement was out, and the people of Chapel Hill were furious.

* * * * *

FURTHER PROVOKING PUBLIC OUTRAGE was President Swain's acceptance of an extravagant gift from none other than General Sherman, the man Southerners most associated with Union atrocities. Upon learning of the engagement of one of his generals to Ella Swain, Sherman sent Swain a horse and carriage to congratulate him.

When Swain and Sherman had met in Raleigh during the surrender of the city, Sherman acknowledged that he knew that Swain was president of the University of North Carolina. The general once had been superintendent of the State Military Academy of Louisiana. The two had taught some of the same students over the years. Their conversation was cordial and ended with Sherman promising to protect Chapel Hill from any harm.

Swain's acceptance of Sherman's gift caused "Southern traditionalists [to] accuse [Swain] of betraying the South," wrote Mrs. Spencer, a gift "which they said must surely have been pillaged from Southern states."

* * * * *

EVEN THOUGH MRS. SPENCER had great admiration for the course the two lovers had chosen, she described the romance as taking place "in the very teeth of all this bitterness and woeful humiliation."

The Swains' neighbors weren't the only ones to object. Citizens across the state were infuriated, believing President Swain had turned his back on their well-being. The university "almost overnight lost many of its old friends and gained a host of powerful enemies," historian William S. Powell wrote in *The First State University*. The impending marriage left the impression that "the University was a center of Unionism and disloyalty, or at the very least of people guilty of fraternizing with the enemy."

Criticism of the courtship also was leveled at General Atkins, whom some Southerners blamed for "the preponderance of Sherman's devastation," Powell wrote. "Far and wide, people suddenly accused him of thievery, even in areas he had never entered."

General Atkins felt he had demonstrated his good faith to Chapel Hill. During the occupation, he ordered his commissary officer to provide rations for any resident, black or white, requesting them. He wrote General Kilpatrick that he was returning "with pleasure" all the animals that had been confiscated "if no campaign is made, believing it would relieve much suffering in this community." Kilpatrick advised him to keep the horses and mules, as they could not be returned "without dismounting men."

Stories of Union soldiers stealing valuables persisted, even though Mrs. Spencer wrote that Chapel Hillians had buried anything worth stealing:

> There was not much provision to be carried off—that was one comfort. The sight of our empty store-rooms and smokehouses would be likely to move our invaders to laughter. Our wardrobes were hardly worth hiding—homespun and jeans hung placidly in their accustomed places.

Atkins became a lightning rod for North Carolinians' anger toward the victorious Union army. Rumors abounded that he had plundered silver and jewelry from North Carolina homes. One of the most widely circulated stories claimed Atkins had taken sterling silver plates from West Hill, the stately Hillsborough home of Rebecca Edwards Jones. Later, her son Dr. Pride Jones was forced to revoke the charge. The theft had, in fact, been committed by one of the Jones's servants and had happened during the encampment at the family's home of Union General Thomas J. Jordan's troops.

Atkins did have his defenders. Governor Graham wrote President Swain in early May that Confederate troops passing through Hillsborough had stolen a mule, several hogs, and all the forage and corn from his plantation. "Gen'l Atkins' provost Marshal sent me a guard the night they spent here, since which time I have had none except my son Augustus, sleeping in the Barn for the protection of my horses."

Even disgruntled merchant Charles Mallett seemed to believe General Atkins was honest, writing his son:

> [Atkins] told Judge Battle yesterday—that he should return home without the slightest evidence of his ever having been south, but his commission that he had not the value of one cent of spoil, and certainly he has used great effort to suppress pillage and wrong.

CHAPTER 4

A General Is Born

TO EASE SOME OF THE ANXIETY he and Eleanor had about their future son-in-law, David Swain traveled to Atkins's home in Freeport, Illinois, 120 miles northwest of Chicago. There, wrote historian Charles Lee Smith, he "satisfied himself as to his [Atkins's] character and social standing." Swain learned that Freeport residents were very proud of the Ninety-second Illinois and General Atkins—the town's only war-time general.

When the Ninety-second arrived home, they were greeted as heroes. The *Freeport Journal* reported the homecoming in its July 19, 1865, issue:

> On Wednesday evening last a large assemblage of our citizens called upon our distinguished fellow citizen, Gen. Smith D. Atkins, for the purpose of expressing to him their warm regard and appreciation of his important service to the country. . . . J. M. Bailey, Esq., delivered an address . . . on behalf of the citizens as follows: "General Atkins—Your neighbors, friends and fellow citizens of Freeport, have assembled here to greet you upon your return to our midst, and it has fallen to my lot to perform the pleasing duty of speaking to you on their behalf, a few words of welcome.

"With pride, to-day, Stephenson county welcomes back her son. After more than four years of distinguished service in the cause of your country, you have at length sheathed the sword and returned to us to engage with us again in the pursuits of peace."

When called on to address the crowd, Atkins thanked those who had gathered to welcome him. In later years, he seldom spoke of his own leadership: "Little have I done to deserve it—none know how little so well as myself—yet I have done what I could." He acknowledged, however, that two acts in his military history made him most proud: enlisting as the first volunteer when Lincoln issued his first call for troops, and re-enlisting when the second call was sounded.

He challenged local residents to build a monument "to the dead heroes of old Stephenson [county], high enough to pierce the clouds, in commemoration of these noble men who have given their lives to gain liberty. . . . I had no wife, no dependent, and my plain duty forced me to go—but no heart can remain unmoved and contemplate the devotion of the rank and file of the American loyal armies."

Believing "a bright future for the country" was possible, he declared, "Blood enough has been shed to give us peace for an hundred years, and I do most earnestly hope that it may be, for I wish never again to look upon the sufferings and devastations of war."

* * * * *

THE ATKINS FAMILY arrived in Freeport in 1848, when Adna Stanly Atkins brought his wife, Sarah Dykins Atkins, and their eleven children, including thirteen-year-old Smith, from New York to what was then a popular frontier shipping town on the Pecatonica River. Adna Atkins opened a tailor shop in a room above the courthouse. A year later, he gave up tailoring and moved his family to a farm.

In Smith Atkins's 1854 journal, he described how the family farm changed over the years:

> [It] looks much more like living now than when my home was on the prairie. The young orchard will bear fruit in a couple of years. . . . the cherry trees, some twenty of them, are large enough now to bear fruit and looking beautifully thrifty. It seems so little a while since I carried those very trees . . . on my back . . . some five miles . . . and now they form a fine row clear around the garden plot. . . . The green prairie that rolled up over the hill from the house has changed now to the dark loam appearance of old proved [*sic*] ground.

He had great fondness for the farm, but no interest in following in his father's footsteps. The newspaper business was his first love, and the legal profession a close second.

At seventeen, he apprenticed at Freeport's first paper, the *Prairie Democrat*, setting type and delivering newspapers. While studying at Rock River Seminary in 1852, he worked as a foreman at the *Mt. Morris*

Gazette to help pay his tuition. A year later, he was reading law with Freeport attorney Hiram Bright and running the *Kane County Democrat.* In spring 1854, he and a friend purchased the *Register* in nearby Savanna, Illinois.

Those days in the newsroom were happy ones, he later noted:

> I worked hard . . . but I was full of glee. . . . It was the hope of the future . . . from journeyman I became a foreman. . . . Then I was editor, the position of honor to the printer apprentice. And if all editors experience the same as I did they will find the editorial sanction to the sum and substance of all glorious, they will find difficulties to meet, trials to encounter, but they can look forward.

Smith Atkins passed the Illinois bar exam in June 1855 and headed to Chicago to work for Judge Grant Goodrich and George Scoville, but he still had not lost his love of newsprint. When typesetters at the *Chicago Tribune* went on strike, he worked there during and after the strike, until the union printers "made it uncomfortable for me in many ways, and, after many weeks, I voluntarily quit."

A year-and-a-half later, he moved home to Freeport. He was twenty-one and ready to practice law on his own. For the next few years, the young attorney distinguished himself as a litigator and politician. He was elected state's attorney on November 6, 1860, the same day Abraham Lincoln was elected president.

The situation between the North and South was unraveling quickly. By mid-December, South Carolina had seceded from the Union. Six more Southern states followed. On April 13, 1861, Confederate forces took over the federal fort at Sumter, South Carolina. Two days later, Lincoln called on young men to enlist in the army to help preserve the United States.

Atkins's eagerness and enthusiasm to serve his country were evident in a July 8, 1861, letter he wrote from Missouri to his law partner's daughter, Winnifred Taylor:

> I hope there will be a chance to fight, I want to go through or fall in a fierce battle before this war ends. I volunteered to fight and I don't want to be cheated out of it. . . . I want to smell gun powder and hear the whistling of leaden balls before I come back again. I think I will. This War must be a fierce one. It may be a long one.

He was not disappointed. In four years of military service, Smith Atkins saw battle time and again, including the bombardment of Fort Henry on the Tennessee River in February 1862 and ten days later at Fort Donelson, Tennessee, where he took sixty-eight men into "this desperate engagement and came out with but twenty-three, having been in the very thickest of the carnage."

In a March 10, 1862, letter to Winnifred's older sister, Lizzie, Atkins admitted he was "indeed fortunate to have passed through it so safely as I did. I now know by experience what a bloody battlefield is . . . what it is to meet the enemy and grapple with him in the death struggle."

During that battle, Captain Atkins suffered from exposure and exhaustion. He was ordered to take sick leave and seriously considered resigning his commission to recover from what he described in a letter to a friend as "my old complaint." But he was suddenly recalled and transferred as acting-assistant adjutant general and clerk to the staff of Brigadier General Stephen A. Hurlbut of the Army of Tennessee.

The division was immediately dispatched to Pittsburgh Landing, Tennessee, where it fought April 6 and 7 at the Battle of Shiloh, deemed by many to have been the bloodiest conflict at that point in the war. Atkins called it "the most awful battle ever fought in the world since the invention of gunpowder."

At the end of the fighting, Hurlbut sent a message to his superior, Captain John A. Rawlins, praising Captain Atkins and recommending he be promoted to major:

> Capt. S.D. Atkins, acting assistant adjutant-general, rose from a sick bed, and was with me until I ordered him to the rear.
>
> He was absent about three hours, and returned and remained throughout the battle.

Atkins's heroic performance forced him to take medical leave. An 1894 sketch of his life, published in the *Freeport Journal*, described him as "impaired by exposure and arduous service in the field." Atkins simply cited the cause for his leave as "ill health."

* * * * *

BACK IN FREEPORT, Atkins got some much-needed rest. But four months later, Lincoln sent out another call for soldiers. Now a major, Atkins rallied and organized a new regiment, the Ninety-second Illinois.

So dire were the needs of the Union army that once he was designated its colonel, the regiment was immediately dispatched to Mount Sterling, Kentucky. There, Atkins was in charge of the first Union regiment to serve that area.

A border state, Kentucky was critical to both sides. It was where brother fought brother and neighbor fought neighbor. It was a state where many prominent citizens spoke out against slavery, but often were hesitant to interfere with the rights of property owners.

No sooner had the Ninety-second arrived than hundreds of slaves inundated its camp "begging for protection, and offering their services to fight for freedom," Atkins later wrote. The slaves were seeking safety from their masters, who wanted them chained and returned.

His superior officer commanded Atkins to return them to the slave owners. Though he disagreed, Atkins issued a general order November 2, 1862, that seemed to address all concerns: It called for owners of slaves to "keep them at home, as no part of my command will in any way be used for the purpose of returning fugitive slaves."

The final section of the order stated that his soldiers would not return slaves to their owners. This "gave us no end of trouble," Atkins recalled. But he remained steadfast in his convictions, declaring, "It is not necessary for Illinois soldiers to become slave-hounds to demonstrate their loyalty, their loyalty has been proved upon too many bloody battlefields to require new proof."

Each night in Mount Sterling, all "colored . . . who were not employed as officer's soldiers would be turned out of camp. Some of them would streak it for the North star, while others would return to their masters."

His own servant was a free black man, born in Wisconsin, "but we were held responsible for every one of our fellow-citizens of African descent who disappeared from the plantations about Mount Sterling." So indignant were local residents that after Atkins's regiment moved on, a circuit court judge convened a special grand jury and indicted the soldiers of the Ninety-second Illinois for stealing.

No action was ever taken to enforce the indictment against the soldiers. "We were not arrested," Atkins explained, "because the sheriff found it inconvenient to take us into custody, there being too many blue-coated soldiers around."

The indictment, he contended, further proved that the South "took up the sword to save slavery, and thereby lost slavery. Those who took up the sword perished by the sword."

Atkins had not always been so vehemently opposed to slavery. As a young man, beginning to develop his own ideas, he wrote in his journal in 1854, "though I . . . despised slavery, I would sober cast my vote for the vainest slave owner, for though I sympathize with the coloured slaves and wish him liberation, I have more sympathy for the white and wish him liberty more."

Although Illinois had been a free state since the adoption of its 1848 constitution, his views changed after he heard abolitionist Frederick Douglass and U.S. Senator Stephen Douglas speak. He finally concluded, "slavery is wrong and I am told the 'honesty is the best policy.' I see no good in it; commercially it is a curse to the country."

In spite of—or perhaps because of—his order at Mount Sterling, Colonel Atkins's personal conduct and performance were rewarded in May 1863 when he was given a regiment command, which included the Ninety-second, under Col. John T. Wilder. They marched across the Cumberland Mountains to Chattanooga, where the battle of Chickamauga was fought on September 19 and 20. At the 1909 Wilder's Brigade Reunion in Effingham, Illinois, he recalled that fierce battle:

> The detail, with all the Spencer rifles in the regiment . . . drove the enemy off the mountain. . . . I have dwelt upon the movements of the Ninety-Second, possibly more than I ought to have. . . . It is a curious fact, disclosed by the Rebellion Records, that the Ninety-Second, not withstanding the terrific fighting on the brigade at Vinyards, lost more men

killed and wounded in the battle of Chickamauga than any
other regiment in Wilder's Brigade.

The horrific conditions forced his men to live on "green chestnuts,
obtained by cutting down the trees and whipping out the burs." They
were willing to eat such sparse rations because they knew others had
nothing to eat, he explained. "That demonstrates the spirit of the
American volunteers. They were all alike."

Such insight was important because conditions did not improve.
Within two months, Atkins and his soldiers fought in the Battle of
Griswoldville, Georgia, and he lamented, "It was a sight never to be
forgotten"—64 men killed and 551 wounded in the first battle of Sherman's March to the Sea.

After an October 4, 1864, battle fought near Powder Springs outside Atlanta, Atkins admitted, "to advance was impossible; to withdraw
might be difficult. . . . The writer does not hesitate to say that he did not
know what to do; disaster appeared inevitable."

Atkins's cavalry brigade continued fighting with Sherman, driv-
ing Confederate soldiers back from Clinton to Macon to Savannah.
There, by order of President Lincoln, Atkins was promoted to brigadier
general for his leadership.

His men next fought at Columbia, South Carolina, in February
1865 and Monroe's Crossroads, North Carolina, in early March. By the
time he led his soldiers at the Battle of Bentonville on March 19, Smith
Atkins had garnered even more praise from his superiors and was made
a major general.

* * * *

DESPITE HIS SUCCESS on the battlefield, Smith Atkins was, by his own account, an unlikely hero. In his late teens and early twenties, he suffered from seasonal depression, bemoaning in his journal, "I don't feel well, nor have felt well all day long. Something ails me." His symptoms were "the blues—bad, very bad . . . down hearted and gloomy. . . . I have no energy." The reasons for "the 'blues' like blazes for two or three days" were unclear, he remarked. "Got them yet. Don't know why."

Even mingling with people seemed an insurmountable task: "Oh, I never was made for society. . . . At least everybody says I am not. Cold, unsociable, morose—disagreeable—Well, if they choose to nag so I cannot help it. I try to be sociable. . . . If people don't like my company. . . . They can just do without . . . and I will do without theirs."

Leadership abilities and friendships, he thought, eluded him:

> Nobody writes to me. My best friends have forgotten me—This world is a frog pond—UGH! UGH! UGH! It seems as though I hadn't got any friends in the world. Dark as thunder. Not a light in the future. No happiness. No nothing. No society— No use of living.

But Smith Atkins the Civil War general displayed none of those doubts or insecurities. Even before the Eleventh Illinois left Freeport in 1861, Atkins and his men were hailed as heroes, according to *In the Footprints of the Pioneers of Stephenson County, Ill.:* "No community exhibited greater patriotism than Stephenson county during the civil war. Scarcely had the smoke at Sumter cleared away before active preparations for war began. . . . All were American for the defence of the country and the flag."

* * * *

THIS WAS THE SMITH Atkins President Swain learned about on his visit to Illinois. He returned home to Chapel Hill bearing good news and bad for his wife, Eleanor. Unfortunately for Mrs. Swain, the general was as intent on the marriage as was Ella. The good news was they would be blessed with financial security. As General Atkins's military service was ending, he had a job waiting—Freeport postmaster, an appointment made by President Lincoln shortly before his assassination.

A postmaster's position would provide the newlyweds an income in a time of economic hardship for so many in the North and the South.

CHAPTER 5

Wedding Vows

ALTHOUGH MRS. SPENCER enjoyed being part of the excitement of wedding planning, she feared that Ella and the general's marriage might damage long-time friendships. She tried to help Ella and the Swain family, despite intimate knowledge of "a good deal of bitter feeling expressed in the village about it all," she wrote in her journal. "The only way one can find an apology for it all is in believing honestly in the love which appears to have brought it about."

President Swain paid no attention to what others had to say, she told Mrs. Swain years later. "About the wedding . . . I think that neither you nor he ever knew to what extent he was blamed. . . . I remember [him] showing me a letter he received to that effect. He would shake his head over such things and let them pass."

A widow who long mourned her husband's death in 1861 (just six years after they wed), Mrs. Spencer placed her loyalties on the side of love. Ella's earlier offhand remark that she had "no fear of being stolen" inspired Mrs. Spencer to write a poem that ended:

> The best artillery is found to be the oldest,
> And peace hath conquests, too, by no means narrow.

The wisest soldier and perchance the boldest,
Yields to a pair of blue eyes and a bow-and-arrow.

Mrs. Spencer had not been particularly enamored of Smith Atkins when they first met. His "short military career," she noted, afforded some "gloss and glamour," and she later confided to Governor Vance that she didn't find the Yankee leader especially well educated and that he "talked through his nose."

On the other hand, when it came to affairs of the heart, she believed the doubters should "think and speak respectfully of a genuine love affair. . . . If this couple truly loves I have no fears for them."

"Amo amantes."

Cherish love.

* * * * *

DURING THE LONG summer days of 1865, Smith Atkins stayed in Freeport, preparing for his job as postmaster and finding a place where he and his bride would live. He also earned a nickname. His wife-to-be now called him "Genl," perhaps out of admiration for her father who, despite his three decades as president of UNC, was still referred to as "Governor" by his friends. To the rest of the world, Smith Atkins was called "General"—the name he would be known by for the rest of his life.

Back in Chapel Hill, Ella busily prepared for their August 23 wedding. There were thank-you notes to write after she showed Mrs. Spencer and her other friends the wedding gifts—"jewelry, books, etc."—Genl's Illinois friends had sent. And there was a bridal gown to be made.

Because money was scarce at that time, brides in the South often had to rework old dresses. Material was prohibitively expensive: "$22 yard for linen . . . $5 apiece for spools of cotton . . . $5 for a paper of pins," Judith W.B. McGuire of Richmond, Virginia, recorded in her diary.

"Of course we used the same style the whole four years of the war in our secluded settlement," Parthenia A. Hague of Alabama wrote in her memoir. "Not a fashion plate or 'ladies' magazine did we see during that entire period, so we were little troubled by the 'latest styles.'"

Mrs. Spencer explained the need for resourcefulness in matters of fashion: "rich and poor fared alike. . . . we boldly invented new fashions and contrivances never before dreamed of. There is nothing like necessity to set people's wits to work."

The Swains sent few invitations for the wedding on August 23, 1865. Unlike Mrs. Spencer, many invitees sent their regrets. "Invitations were spit upon in one or two houses!" she wrote, adding that some family friends "were very hot against Ellie."

* * * * *

B Y ALL REPORTS, Ella was a beautiful bride, entering the Swains' parlor at eight o'clock that warm summer evening to the piano strains of favorite hymns. She wore a white grosgrain silk bodice and skirt that accented her dark, shoulder-length hair and blue eyes.

Attending the ceremony were former Governor Graham and his wife, Susan. Both seem to have been fond of the groom. Until his death in 1875, Governor Graham corresponded with Atkins; and his son, John W. Graham, was called on to defend the Union general against highly charged rumors that he had plundered silver and jewels from local homes. "I regret very much that there can be found a person in North Carolina who will descend so low for the purpose of injuring the University," John Graham wrote President Swain about the maligning of his new son-in-law. "It really seems to me sometimes that a portion of our Southern people have lost all common sense in regard to the nation."

Also present were some UNC faculty and their families, as well as "a number of gallant ex-Confederate soldiers," Union army officers, a few close friends, and Mrs. Spencer's brother, Samuel Phillips, who had served as auditor for Governor Vance's Confederate government. Certainly sharing in the festivities would have been Ella's sister, Anne, her brother, Bunkey, and his wife and young daughter, her mother's sisters—Emma, Susan, Betsy, and Sophronia—and Sophronia's husband, John.

Officiating was the Reverend Dr. Fordyce M. Hubbard, a longtime family friend and Chapel of the Cross rector. When he called for anyone who could "show just cause, why they may not lawfully be joined together, let him now speak, or else hereafter for ever hold his peace," no one stepped forward.

Reciting from the 1789 Book of Common Prayer, Dr. Hubbard asked General and Ella if they would love, comfort, and forsake all others "so long as ye both shall live?"

Family and friends looked on as the couple, standing upon a Brussels carpet—one of the Swain family's prized possessions—responded, "I will."

Even as Ella and General recited their vows, anger about the marriage was not subdued. For three long hours that evening, university students tolled the campus bells in protest and hung General Atkins and President Swain in effigy from the bell tower of Old South, the university's main building.

The bell-ringing did not interrupt the ceremony. The marriage was sealed when General Smith Atkins placed on Ella Swain's left hand the wedding ring—a filigree band topped with a miniature crown of dozens of tiny, shiny diamonds.

A grand supper followed, despite food shortages caused by the war and its aftermath. Guests dined on some of the Swains' favorite dishes—turkey salad, scalloped oysters, greens, and summer fruits.

It was the wedding cake, "large and handsomely decorated," Mrs. Spencer wrote, that truly stood out in the lavish feast. A gift from the freedmen, former slaves who had been liberated after the Civil War, the cake was given to "their deliverer and liberator," in Mrs. Spencer's words. Reviled by some, the general was a hero to others. Emblematic of the rapidly changing world in which they were living, the guests ate the cake baked by these newly freed slaves, as the loud protest continued from Old South.

The newlyweds and guests "spent the evening pleasantly," and Mrs. Spencer found herself acknowledging the event "passed off very well, whatever we might think of it. . . . General Atkins is a handsome man, rather grave in expression, sedate and courteous in manner. Elly looked well—beautifully dressed."

Later in the evening, Dr. Hubbard recorded the marriage in the church's daily log: *Brig. Gen. Smith D. Atkins, of Freeport, Illinois, to Miss Eleanor H. Swain, daughter of Gov. D.L. Swain.*

* * * * *

THE NEWLYWEDS REMAINED in Chapel Hill for a week. They were honored at two parties, given by old friends of Mrs. Swain—Sarah Cox Fetter and Martha H. Hubbard. However, furor over the marriage was evident in the scant notice it received in local newspapers. One would have expected the wedding of the daughter of the University of North Carolina president and former North Carolina governor, and great-granddaughter of the state's first governor, to be a major news story. But the event garnered little more than a mention in the September 3 issue of the *Raleigh Sentinel.*

In contrast, Illinois papers didn't shy away from covering the wedding of a favorite son. The September 27 issue of the *Freeport Journal* claimed its tongue-in-cheek account of the wedding was reprinted "From a Southern paper":

> General Smith D. Atkins, of Freeport, Illinois, who accompanied the victorious armies of the Union into this department, made an important capture on the 23rd Aug., at Chapel Hill, in the person of Miss Eleanor H. Swain, the accomplished daughter of Hon. David L. Swain, ex-Governor of North Carolina, who presented the General with his prize which was pronounced a valid conquest by Rev. Dr. Hubbard, in the presence of a large number of officers of the army, and distinguished citizens of the state.
>
> It is expected that other captures of a similar character will be made in this department by distinguished Union officers, who have been fighting it out on that line all summer.

* * * * *

A FTER THE WEDDING, Mrs. Spencer wrote a defense of the marriage, hoping others would "think and speak respectfully of a genuine love-affair. Since the world began, it has been a wonderful agent for good, sometimes for evil, but true love has done more good than harm. If this couple truly Love each other I have no fears for them. . . ."

Yet, she never made her declarations public.

Outrage about the marriage continued. It built upon the general unease many felt toward President David Swain, who had been a late and somewhat reluctant supporter of the Confederate cause. According to Mrs. Spencer, he "never entertained extreme views in regard to 'State Rights,' and did not permit himself to become embittered against the North during the War. . . . his forbearance was even clearer afterwards."

At the time of his daughter's wedding, he also was caught up in the volatile politics of Reconstruction: A state constitutional convention was set to convene to discuss, among other topics, the future of the university—from its president and faculty, to its leadership model, and its desperate need for financial relief.

Regardless of one's point of view, the university's long-time president had become an easy target for condemnation. A *Raleigh Sentinel* reporter wrote that the university was reviled on one side for being a "Yankee concern" and on the other for being "a hot-bed of rebellion."

Mrs. Spencer believed President Swain should have spoken out and defended himself and the university. But, she noted, he "was supremely indifferent to the gossip and scandal."

When he showed her letters berating him for permitting his daughter to marry a Yankee general, "he would shake his head and say, 'No need to correct such things.'"

When she suggested he allow her to "tell all about it some day to the papers," President Swain replied, "When I am dead, you may."

CHAPTER 6

The Wide-Awake Life

A T THE END of August, the newlyweds left Chapel Hill and spent a month traveling to their new home in Illinois. They visited New York City and Chicago before arriving in Freeport. It was Ella's first time outside North Carolina.

In Freeport, Ella felt a sense of adventure and excitement. With a population of 8,300, it was a bustling city—its main streets lined with shops, churches, a concert hall, an armory, and a firehouse. In contrast, Chapel Hill was a quiet village existing solely to serve the university, with a population (including students) of fewer than 1,000.

The couple initially lived at Brewster House, Freeport's finest hotel. A few days after arriving, Ella wrote her parents and Anne on October 3:

> Here I am in our pleasant little private parlor attached
> to our bedroom. . . . I feel very cosy just now—sitting as
> I am, by my little marble top table with my lamp, books &
> fragrant flowers on it, & the Genl with his newspaper & cigar
> sitting opposite me, a bright fire in the stove & moonlight
> & gass light making the street look bright & full of life
> thro my window, while the constant whistle of trains coming
> & going & the continual passing on the street gives strong

evidence of the thrift & progress of the city. . . . Freeport
bids fair to become one of the flourishing city's of the Union.
How unlike the sleep & perfect quiet, which pervades
my own beloved South, is the hurry & wide awake life of
the North.

Brewster House, with its fifty-one rooms, overlooked the city's
two main thoroughfares. Abraham Lincoln and Stephen Douglas had
stayed there during one of their senate debates in the 1850s.

Their quarters were on the third floor, which had nine parlors with
bedrooms and the ladies' water closet. Ella didn't think they would be
there long:

> Genl has prevailed on Mr. Krinbill [Atkins's sister Cynthia's
> husband], who is one of the best men, to make an addition to
> his house of three rooms & let us live with them. . . .We hope
> to be able to take up our quarters there in about a month. It is
> so good in them to build just to oblige us!

Hoping to reassure her parents of her husband's generosity, Ella
described gifts she had received from him, gifts that were truly appreci-
ated after years of scarcity:

> You ought to see my pretty new shoes with coral buttons &
> crimson chemille tassles [sic] "my good husband" gave me
> tonight, & the nice warm knit shirts & drawers. He gets
> them all himself & is never more delighted than when he can
> throw an armfull of bundles into my lap. It is like living in
> fairyland after our four long years privation. . . .

Missing from Ella's first letter was mention of her upcoming twenty-third birthday. For that occasion, Genl gave her a Bible inscribed with their names and a prayer: *A guide to life eternal, O, May it lead us there.*

The letter also did not mention her health: Ella was pregnant.

* * * * *

H APPY AS THEY WERE, the newlyweds were not spared the volatility of post-Civil War America. Politics prevented Atkins from immediately starting his job as postmaster. There was grumbling in Washington that he was a less-than-ardent supporter of Lincoln's successor, Andrew Johnson. Atkins was an active member of the Republican Party, and Illinois Republicans were losing patience with Johnson, a Jacksonian Democrat.

Republicans were particularly upset by the president's support of a bill that would require freedmen to pass a literacy test before they could be eligible to vote. Johnson also failed to support the Freedmen's Bureau, charged with helping ex-slaves find jobs and homes and establishing schools, churches, and hospitals. Further, he had appointed white loyalists to head provisional governments in Southern states. Throughout the region, legislatures passed Black Codes, dramatically restricting the freedoms of former slaves and requiring them to work or be arrested. This often meant that freedmen had to return to the fields and work for wages so low they were forced to live in poverty.

Atkins later would note in the margin of *A Constitutional View of the Late War Between the States, Its Causes, Character, Conduct & Results* (a book published in 1870 by Alexander H. Stephens, vice president of the Confederacy):

> I was with the Army in North Carolina at the time, and expressed the opinion, which I still hold, that President Johnson had not one particle of authority under the Constitution of the United States to appoint a Provisional Government, or a Provisional Judge of a court.

Never one to shy away from expressing his beliefs, he must have made his views public enough that Johnson, a thousand miles away, delayed replacing Freeport's sitting postmaster until late that fall.

Earning a living was important—Atkins had responsibility for supporting his new family. During the political maneuvering, he returned to law, opening a practice with Colonel George Hicks. According to the *Freeport Journal,* "General Atkins is too widely known to require introduction at our hands, and with his associate, will undoubtedly take first rank among the professional men of acknowledged ability of our city."

* * * * *

A S ELLA'S PREGNANCY PROGRESSED, she went into confinement—a social convention that kept visibly pregnant women housebound and out of the public eye—in their new home in the recently completed addition to the Krinbills' house.

On June 21, 1866, nearly ten months after the Atkinses's wedding day, the couple welcomed a boy, Swain Graham Atkins. Tragically, Baby Graham lived just one day.

In mourning, Ella found her husband sensitive and understanding. She also relied on the comfort of friends and parishioners from Zion Episcopal Church, where they worshipped and Atkins served on the vestry. But she longed for her family.

Shortly after their first wedding anniversary, Ella and the general traveled to Chapel Hill. Time had not diminished the hostility some felt toward the couple. "Most persons think it a great pity she should come home at all in such a crisis in our affairs," Mrs. Spencer wrote her friend, Mrs. J.J. Summerell of Salisbury. "General Atkins and Ellie coming here this fall has increased the bitterness."

The intervening year had not been an easy one in Chapel Hill. The state's Constitutional Convention of 1865 had determined that North Carolina's pre-war debt had to be repaid, but its wartime obligations did not. This was a particular blow to the university. During the war, it had invested in bank stock and Confederate securities, all of them now worthless.

The university was broke. President Swain was forced to spend much of his time trying to find adequate funding to keep its doors open. University trustees sent him North to attempt to mortgage university property. But even wealthy New Yorker financier John Jacob Astor III wouldn't take a chance on North Carolina real estate.

The university's financial picture grew so dire that even faculty salaries were in arrears. "Chapel Hill people are very poor . . . all so dependent on the prosperity of the University," Mrs. Spencer wrote. "Its decline carries the whole village down."

Further complicating the situation was an incident that spring when students planning the university's commencement ball printed invitations listing their choice of guests of honor: former Confederate President Jefferson Davis, Confederate Generals W.R. Cox, J.C. Breckinridge, Robert D. Johnston, and Robert E. Lee, and the state's Confederate Governor Zebulon B. Vance.

The timing was a disaster. The students had not consulted President Swain or the trustees, who had to approve all honorees. But word of the unauthorized action got out.

"President Swain and his staff were thrown into . . . almost a panic," Kemp Battle wrote. They feared that the U.S. Congress, deeply suspicious of the South, might retaliate with "hostile legislation."

Other Carolinians were also concerned. With only three seniors graduating and school coffers empty, there were veiled calls for Swain's resignation. Federal governor and newspaper editor W.W. Holden denounced the university as a "center of aristocracy and rebellion."

One of the students' honorary guests, former Governor Vance, was officially invited as a commencement speaker. As popular after the war as before, he gave a rousing address, "The Duties of Defeat."

"Everything went off well," wrote Mrs. Spencer.

Yet the controversy lingered.

Ella and the general's first trip home only fueled the anger of President Swain's detractors, leading to more calls for his resignation—even, it seems, from Mrs. Spencer, who wrote Mrs. Summerell, "Everybody agrees that the Governor [Swain] must resign, or the University is doomed, yet nobody will tell him so."

But President Swain had no intention of stepping down and "continued to labor with all his former energy," wrote Battle. "Never did an officer give his whole heart and anxious care to the interests of his charge more devotedly than he . . . the students were his children."

Ella didn't seem to notice these problems. Nor did she sense any coldness directed at her, her husband, or her father. In fact, when it was time to leave, she decided to extend her stay. General Atkins returned home alone and was not with his bride that October on her twenty-fourth birthday. Instead, he mailed her a birthday poem, which in part read:

> Happy day, happy day, Baby, dear;
> Throw life's sorrow all away, Baby, dear.
> Happy day, and happy year, And many happy days and years!
> Lay the old year on his bier, Shedding only joyful tears . . .
> As we journey on our way, Baby, dear,
> Let us drop a silent tear, on the grave of the old year;
> Then look forward without fear, All the future's bright and clear,
> Baby, dear.

The poem spoke volumes to all that had taken place in recent months: Baby Graham had died four months earlier, and they were anticipating the birth of another child, for Ella was three months pregnant. Fearing that Freeport's harsh winter had contributed to the death of her first child, she wanted to remain in Chapel Hill.

General visited her in November, then again sent her poetry as a New Year's gift—this time a copy of Oliver Goldsmith's mournful poem, "The Deserted Village." Inscribed to *Mrs. Eleanor H. Atkins with love of Smith D. Atkins,* the eighteenth-century poem tells of the destruction of a village, as the promise of wealth lures its children elsewhere.

He found significance in some of its lines, which he marked lightly in pencil:

> Ill fares the land to hastening ills a prey,
> Where wealth accumulates, and men decay;
> Princes and lords may flourish, or may fade;
> A breath can make them, as a breath has made;
> But a bold peasantry, their country's pride,
> When once destroyed, can never be supplied.

Perhaps he read Goldsmith's classic poem as a cautionary tale about a community lost, about class struggle, about the sorrow of a family divided.

CHAPTER 7

Anne

A MONG THE PEOPLE drawing Ella back to Chapel Hill was Anne, her older sister who had never married and lived with the Swains at the President's House on Franklin Street. Life had not been easy for Anne. She had suffered many illnesses during her thirty-seven years.

In early winter of 1867, however, it was Ella's health that preoccupied the Swains. In her second trimester, Ella was "quite unwell at intervals," President Swain wrote Governor William Graham, observing that neither of his daughters seemed "to have the hardihood they ought to have inherited."

By midwinter, with Ella in the last months of her pregnancy, everyone's focus shifted to Anne. She had grown noticeably weak and become gravely ill. The diagnosis was grim: Anne had breast cancer, a disease that in 1867 usually carried with it a dire prognosis.

* * * * *

ANNE WAS TWO YEARS OLD when David Swain
became governor of North Carolina in December 1832 and
the family moved into the "Governor's Palace" in Raleigh.
Already her father was expressing concern about her health: "Poor little
Anna is ever present to my thoughts," he had written his wife while he
was traveling around the state.

In Raleigh, the Swains were near White Hall, the home of Anne's
maternal grandmother, Anna Caswell White, as well as her aunts
Emma, Sophronia, and Susan. All of them helped with Anne and
were a comfort to the Swains, especially when their second child, baby
David, died that summer, leaving Anne an only child until December
1834, when another son, "Little David," was born.

After Swain was elected president of the University of North Carolina in late 1835, at the end of his third term as governor, the family
moved to Chapel Hill.

This new position allowed the Swains to finally put down roots.
Growing up in Chapel Hill, Anne, Little David, and Richard (Bunkey,
born in 1837) spent their days playing with the children of both faculty
and townspeople.

Anne's childhood was often disturbed by illness. She suffered from
an anxiety disorder that was never fully understood. Possibly it was
exacerbated by the losses the Swains experienced, particularly the unexpected death of five-year-old Little David a week after Anne's eleventh
birthday. Two years later, her infant sister, named Ella, died only a few
days before the birth of a new baby, also named Ella (who would grow
up to marry General Smith Atkins).

Despite ill health, Anne was "always affectionate, generous, charitable, humble," noted Mrs. Spencer. In her February 27, 1845, journal entry, she recorded:

> Mary Hall, Anne Swain and I having picked each other up at intervals along the way, fell in at Mrs. Fetter's the other day. While there, conducted a most edifying conversation. . . .

By her early twenties, Anne was being treated for insanity and occasionally needed to be institutionalized. Her family hoped each such occurrence would be the last. "I hope your sister Anne's health continues to improve," Aunt Betsy wrote her nephew Bunkey in 1853, "and when I get to Raleigh I shall find her the same cheerful creature she used to be in bygone days."

When Mrs. Swain's cousin Richard Gatlin of St. Louis learned of Anne's illness, he wrote that he regretted the toll it was taking on the Swains: "How very much distressed her parents must be." He mentioned Anne's condition to his friend, Episcopalian Bishop Cicero Hawks, who "told me that it was frequently the case that insanity was proceeded by the formation of matter at the root of the brain. . . . I do hope that dear Annie will in time be relieved."

During Anne's hospitalization in 1854, Mrs. Swain received a letter from her friend, Mary E. Hooper:

> I was with you long ago and shared your grief when you lost your "little ones." I can remember you saying that "if those trials did not bring you to the Savior nothing ever would." I cannot realize that this last bitter affliction is greater than they were. . . . I always loved Annie from a child and can and shall remember with pleasure her sweet gentle manners. . . . tell me how she is, and if you can do so send her my love.

In January 1856, David Swain went to see his daughter, who once again had been institutionalized. After the visit, Mrs. Swain wrote to Anne that her Pa had never seen her "look so well and cheerful." She complimented her daughter on an essay she had written entitled, "A Voice from Work House, Hospital & Jail," and praised her "spirit of inspiration." But Anne responded with a description of herself as "a poor child . . . my heart is full of earnest love for you and I often, often think of you."

Anne also suffered from chronic excruciating headaches, perhaps related to her mental illness. Desperate to numb the pain, she turned to using opium, one of the few pain relievers she found effective. She grew poppies in the Swains' backyard in Chapel Hill and harvested the colorful flowers' seedpods for opium, a remedy that was not uncommon in the mid-nineteenth century. It was legally sold in various forms but was in short supply because of the war.

Her Aunt Susan though advised against this treatment, explaining in a March 1857 letter, "I am no advocate of opiate or stimulants, they will ease pain but aggravate diseases, this has long been my opinion." Susan had experience to support her opinion. Her sister, Emma, occasionally used opiates, as she reminded her niece:

> Emma says she will never use morphine again if she can help it, only in violent attacks where nothing else will do, she seems convinced it is the cause of the difficulty of breathing she has.

Despite Susan's pleas, Anne continued using opium, a treatment fully supported by her doctor. Though she didn't always follow her aunts' advice, they held a special place in her life. She frequently visited Susan and Emma in Raleigh, and Betsy White Felton in La Grange, near

Kinston. Interestingly, the severity of her headaches was often dramatically reduced while she stayed with her mother's sisters.

* * * * *

ANNE'S ILLNESSES weighed heavily on the Swain family. In early 1862, Mrs. Swain wanted nothing more for her eldest child than relief. She wrote to her friend Selina Wheat:

> Poor Anna still suffers very much. I have very little hope that
> it will be otherwise with the close of this life and then I hope
> her suffering will end in a glorious immortality.

That her final suffering was not caused by the mental infirmity she had battled for decades made little difference. In the weeks following the diagnosis of breast cancer, Anne's illness was "a source of much anxiety," President Swain wrote to Governor Graham. She was "so very unwell in body and mind, that I dare not leave home today."

Bunkey arrived in Chapel Hill in mid-March with his wife, Maggie, and their three-year-old Lula.

For the last time, all three Swain siblings were under the same roof.

Bunkey and Maggie offered some relief to Ella and Mrs. Swain, who "did not close her eyes last night, and is so much wearied, worried and exhausted," her husband told Mrs. Spencer. Mrs. Swain was so devoted to her first-born, she would hardly leave Anne's room, President Swain confided.

Ella also stayed close to her much-loved sister, nursing her as well as her own health would allow. President Swain tried to protect his younger daughter from Anne's approaching death, advising her "not to go into the sick room," but she could not stay away. In Ella's presence, "Anne was better and I was grateful she did not take my advice," he told Mrs. Spencer.

Mrs. Swain, according to her husband, "was all the time at her [Anne's] side, and during the last 36 hours realized" their daughter soon would die.

Their hope for an end to suffering and "a glorious immortality" came for Anne in the early evening of Tuesday, March 26, 1867.

During her funeral held two days later at Chapel of the Cross Episcopal Church, where she had been a member, Anne was granted one of her last wishes, according to Mrs. Spencer:

> Dying, she asked that the colored people should sing a certain hymn at her grave, and this they did, many of them in tears as their simple melody rose in the air.

Anne was buried in the family's backyard garden—where she once had grown poppies—beside the grave of her brother, David, and sister "Infant Ella."

CHAPTER 8

Life on Prospect Terrace

SMITH ATKINS, WHO HAD traveled to Chapel Hill for Anne's funeral, stayed on with Ella, awaiting the birth of their second child. Three weeks after Anne died, David Swain Atkins was born on April 21 at eight in the morning.

When the Atkins family returned to Freeport and their new two-story house on Prospect Terrace, Ella was busy settling in and caring for her "most beautiful baby," her "father's most worthy namesake." Still eager to reassure her parents that she had married the right man, Ella wrote about Genl's devotion to his son:

> He makes every thing move in accordance with the will of his lordly little Swain & he returns his Father's attentions by his first word being "Papa" . . . Genl keeps the crib on his side of the bed because he is afraid I will not wake at Davids call so soon as he does & often can rock him to sleep again without waking me at all & then he keeps fire & light burning all night so that the young Prince can have every thing comfortable at any time he wishes to get up & have a promenade.

Her husband often rocked David before bedtime. Ella described the scene of "the dearest little boy in all the world . . . now in Genl's arms singing as Genl talks him to sleep." One Sunday while David's nurse was at church, Atkins took over the baby's care:

> Genl has David trying every means to amuse him. . . . I do wish you could see David now on the bed flat on his back his face stuck in a tin pail & Genls drumming on the bottom with a stick to the great delight of the young Gov. . . . [He] is so full of mischief. He will try to imitate his Papa smoke & everything else he sees him or any one else do. . . . David has five teeth now & can stand alone says "Bye Bye" & jabbers constantly; oh how sweet his mouth looks filled almost in front with mild white teeth & oh how he bites me but I have not slapped him. . . . He is much more fond of his Papa than me. . . .

Ella was proud of her son—"my hired girls are delighted & what have I to do but be full of joy myself"—and told her father "the care of your mischievous namesake keeps me well employed & gives but little time for anything else."

General Atkins had a lot to balance. In addition to his duties as postmaster and his law practice, he attended to many civic duties. He was a supporting member of the Freeport Fire Department (participating in its annual parade and ball) and chairman and recording secretary of the Stephenson County Soldiers' Monument Association, the memorial he had proposed when he returned home from war. He also helped organize the first reunion of the members of the Ninety-second Illinois.

With a baby and new home to care for, Ella too was busy. Learning to run a household was a challenge for a young Southern woman who had been raised in a household with slaves. Now Ella relied on a "hired girl" and a nurse for David. Expressing surprise at "the difference between Northern & Southern help," Ella wrote that she felt "very fortunate in the way of hired help which is a matter of great importance among house keepers here as good help is very scarce."

She believed her parents would understand the importance of all the chores her helper performed:

> These things from any one else my dear Pa would come very small to you but as they come from your child I believe you will be smiles . . . she is a first class cook baking deserts [*sic*] cakes soups & all kinds of cookery I never ate. She does the washing for the entire family my nurse included . . . & David's alone is about four times as large as your house hold & change of bed clothes for three beds every week & table linen . . . makes fires all over the house before we are up, does all our marketing, waits on table & helps me sew & any thing else that comes in the way & the kitchen is just as clean as my parlor.

Ella considered herself to be a "a very industrious housekeeper," complimented by her friends "for keeping a first class table." At the same time, she was economical:

> My hired girl said . . . she "never lived with any lady who seemed to understand so well how to save & at the same time to set so good a table that she did not see that even a cold potato had found its way to the swill pail."

She paid the worker $8 per month, "$2.00 less on the wage than she received from any former place."

Despite her thrift, Ella soon wrote home for money, finding herself "obliged to try & help Genl pay for our little home, unless <u>Pa</u> can aid us which I am satisfied he will do if he can I scarce know how we can meet our payments." Her parents would understand that "it was indispensable that we should have a home of our own with our baby & nurse." She assured them the house was "small & plain just as small as we could get along with comfort & just as plain as people moving in the society that we do would like to welcome our friends to & extravagance has had no hand in it but only an eye to comfort & quality."

How President Swain responded isn't known. But another source of help was on the way: After nearly twenty years on their farm, Atkins's elderly parents had decided to move in with their son and daughter-in-law, and help with the finances. "They refuse to live with their children unless they pay board," Ella explained. In their mid-seventies, the senior Atkinses suffered from ailments brought on by years of hard work. Ella described them as "both failing fast every day & what keeps her alive I can't see for she is a skeleton & every coughing spell she has seems as if it would take her away. She can't walk without aid & cant turn her self in bed."

As a young man, Atkins had confided in his journal:

> Mother is quite unwell. . . . Age is fast wearing upon her, her health is growing feeble and at best it cannot be long before the rider on the pale horse will come to my home and my aged parents will be borne away. . . . I wish I was worth a good fortune that I might give it to my parents . . . [to] spend their old age in a little more sunny-like [environ].

Now he was able to do just that.

Ella wrote her parents, "Grand Pa and Grand Ma . . . seem very much delighted and I am pleased to have it in my power to contribute my share towards making them comfortable. . . ."

The added responsibility did not seem to distract her from home-making. She and the cook frequently tried "Ma's receipts [recipes] very successfully & afforded me much satisfaction as a reminder of other days at home." Among her favorites were spring radishes and lobster salad with young spring lettuce, "grown in a hothouse."

Though Sarah Atkins was infirm, Ella probably benefited from her cooking advice. While in college, Smith had written in his journal that his mother was "just the very best cook in the world. . . . Brother and I are going out home tomorrow. A pretty good walk, ten miles—but it will give me a good appetite and my good mother will cook for us the very best of good things to eat."

* * * * *

AMILY LIFE WAS FULL. Not only was the Prospect Terrace house brimming with three generations of Atkinses, but Ella's brother, Bunkey Swain, now lived only fifteen miles away in Shannon and was a frequent guest.

For Bunkey, it had been a long road to Illinois.

Following his 1858 graduation from UNC, he attended Jefferson Medical College in Philadelphia, though he stayed just one semester. News of John Brown's raid on Harpers Ferry in late 1859 prompted two hundred Southern students to walk out of medical school in protest of what they considered to be federal support for the anti-slavery movement.

Many of the young men transferred to Southern medical schools. Bunkey enrolled at the Medical College of South Carolina in Charleston.

When the Southern states seceded in spring 1861, Bunkey's education again was interrupted. Without a medical degree, and with a war looming and no prospects for starting his own practice, he returned to Chapel Hill. At twenty-three, his future looked bleak.

President Swain, however, had a job for him. Months earlier, Mrs. Swain's widowed sister Ann (Nancy) died in Shelbyville, Tennessee. Bunkey was sent to help with the estate and check on land the Swains owned that had been managed by Nancy's late husband, Daniel L. Barringer.

Bunkey did more than check on family real estate. He fell in love. On June 9, 1861, he married Shelbyville native Susan E. Burt. In a letter to Selina Wheat, Mrs. Swain described her new daughter-in-law as "pretty and a good woman, but her health is very frail."

The newlyweds moved to Weldon, North Carolina, where Bunkey worked as an apprentice in a medical practice. Under the supervision of Chapel Hill physicians William P. Mallett and Johnston B. Jones, he finally had received his medical license.

Unfortunately, Mrs. Swain's comments about Susan's frailty were all too true. Less than a year after they married, Susan died of consumption. Just weeks before, Anne Swain had written to Mrs. Spencer that a family friend was creating a cameo of "my poor brother's wife."

Grief-stricken, Bunkey left his medical practice and joined the Thirty-ninth Regiment North Carolina Infantry, organized in Asheville by his cousin, Colonel David Coleman. The regiment was assigned to Knoxville, Tennessee, where it guarded bridges, supplies, and communication lines along the railroad.

As an assistant surgeon, Bunkey experienced the horrors of war. His regiment was involved in fighting that resulted in "frightful losses," its doctors being "overwhelmed" by the carnage and the "endless lines of men needing amputation," wrote historian Gordon Phillips.

By late fall, Bunkey was assigned to a hospital in Shelbyville, the very town where he had met his late wife. Once again he fell in love with a Shelbyville woman. He and Margaret (Maggie) Louisa Steele were married on January 6, 1863. They lived in Shelbyville, where their daughter, Eleanor Louise (Lula), was born on November 2.

As the war continued, Bunkey had trouble establishing a medical practice. Possibly compounding his difficulties were signs that he was suffering from what now is called post-traumatic stress disorder from his war experience. In a November 1865 letter, Mrs. Swain's cousin Mary Gatlin acknowledged, "I'm sorry to hear of Richard's disappointments in life. . . . I hope by this time he's doing a good business."

After Bunkey, Maggie, and Lula traveled to Chapel Hill shortly before Anne's death, they stayed with the Swains for several months. Later that year, Bunkey moved to Illinois, accepting General Atkins's offer to help him set up a medical practice. He left Maggie and Lula with his parents until he was established.

In her letters home, Ella hinted at Bunkey's possible drinking problem, but also expressed pride in her brother's success:

> [It] will give pleasure to every one . . . [to] hear the most pleasing reports from Bunk "perfectly sober attending to his business and plenty business to do." He has written us quite often of late but has only been to see us twice since Christmas. . . . And tho we are ever glad to see him . . . he is where he should be at his post attending to his profession.

* * * * *

ELLA WAS HAPPY to have family nearby, especially when Maggie and Lula finally joined Bunkey. She wrote her mother about visiting them: "I went with [Genl] as far as Shannon & spent the day with Mag & met Genl at the train . . . in the afternoon & came home bringing Mag & Lula with us."

That Friday evening, Ella wrote:

> I had all of Genls family that could come to dine with Mary Bell (Genl's niece who just married) at my house. & besides Mag and Lula there were present Uncle Isac & Aunt Milley Bechtol, Lula Welch & child, Margaret Hawley & two children, Mary & her husband Mr. Swartz & I had of his family a married brother & wife & two single brothers.

She enjoyed entertaining, especially for holidays when she prepared the recipes she remembered from home:

> I had for dinner . . . an enormous Turkey & splendid roast of vinsom [sic] & stewed oisters [sic], turnips, sweet & Irish potatoes, onions boiled, hot slaw, stewed tomatoes, cranberry sauce, fruit jelly, Celery pickles, light bread, french rolls tea & coffee. For desert [sic] mince pies, boiled custard, coconut pudding, iced cake, tarts & candy & all said it was a splendid dinner. I am getting quite a name up as a housekeeper I tell you I am & your receipts [recipes] are borrowed by all my friends.

Opportunities to prove herself a good wife, homemaker, and mother were important to Ella. Like most women of that day, she made her family's clothes. She wrote Mrs. Swain that she was busy "sewing . . . articles which were needed like canton flannel drawers for my self, the completion of shirts for Genl & hence my neglect of writing often to my own dear Mamy."

Occasionally she splurged on a special outfit; but she pointed out that she made it herself instead of paying a dressmaker:

> I have made . . . a very handsome suit for my self of poplin Alpaca dress & shirt saque very handsomely trimmed goared skirt trimmed with three folds of the same put on in festoons with an ornament at the end of each festoon. . . . The dress maker said she had made at least 40 dresses of the same material since Christmas. . . . They have it of every colour & tis the most popular goods in the market now & costs only 73 cents per yard.

Ella's correspondence was newsy, but seldom addressed politics. Things were contentious in 1868 with the impeachment of President Andrew Johnson. Her letters didn't mention that her husband had broken with the Republican Party and opposed Johnson's impeachment, causing some to question Atkins's suitability to continue serving as postmaster.

In one letter she admitted to her father that she had a soft spot for the North Carolina-born Johnson:

> There is of course a good deal of feeling at present as regards the impeachment of Mr. Johnson. Being as well acquainted with the political feeling of North-South & being a woman

> I don't feel as if I can take either side, but I can say that from
> my personal knowledge of the President I am very much dis-
> posed to feel very kindly towards my P.M. which stands for
> both Poor Man as well as Post master.

Though many Northerners were unhappy with the conciliatory ideas
of the Southern-born-and-bred president, Ella knew David Swain
would understand. When President Johnson attended the university's
1867 commencement, he received a warm welcome. The Swains hosted
a reception in his honor, with "a rich and bountiful table . . . loaded with
all good things of the season . . . apples, bananas, oranges, filberts."

Later lauded as the only Illinois postmaster to support Johnson,
Atkins was reappointed by every president, except Grover Cleveland,
the lone Democratic president during the general's tenure.

* * * * *

MARRIAGE AND MOTHERHOOD brought Ella
joy. But she longed for her North Carolina family. She
missed her late sister, writing her mother on the anniversary of Anne's death:

> All day yesterday . . . I sat with you in memory by the
> death bed on that one year deserted chamber of our
> loved . . . "Gentle Anne" at the moment of her departure.
> I suffered with you, all of today my eyes have rested on the
> face of the quiet sleeper, & like that day one year ago, my
> eyes are dry. A stern grief that finds no solace a deep grief
> that keeps fresh & will keep so thro years of change.

The family all felt that stern grief. Every day, President Swain visited his eldest daughter's grave in the family garden.

Ella's letters were filled with reminiscences about her family. She wrote in March 1868, "How often, Pa, I call to mind our old frolicsome 'good night' and it comes very sadly 'over the hills and far aways.'"

CHAPTER 9

My Desolate Home

THOUGH SHE STILL mourned Anne, Ella's happiness seemed abundant. She and Genl had a beautiful son, a lovely home, financial security, and each other. In March 1868, she wrote her parents that "our David" had seven new teeth and was trying all sorts of foods including "large potatoes with steak gravy a slice of bread & butter large baked apple & cup of coffee . . . & he nurses as much as if he had no other food."

Like many young children, David got sick at times and at one point had "not been very well for days, his bowels being the cause of trouble brought on by his teeth," she explained. However, his bouts with various ailments did not seem to be cause for alarm.

Thus it came as a deep shock when on June 3, 1868, little David died. He was, according to his obituary, "1 year, 1 month, and 19 days old."

Quite possibly, he had succumbed to an affliction known as "second summer disease," a digestive disorder that struck newly weaned children during the warm months. According to an 1882 medical encyclopedia, "The second summer [in a child's life] is regarded with awe and fear amounting to superstition. In fact, public opinion looks for a higher mortality in the second than in the first summer."

The theory behind second summer disease had to do with the introduction of cow's milk into the toddler's diet. In some children, milk caused digestive problems that could lead to dysentery, which—if not successfully treated—caused the child to quickly become dehydrated and die.

* * * * *

"MY DESOLATE HOME," began Ella's letter to her parents following the tragedy:

> I've nothing to write about, no messages from our David, oh my task is finished. I've no work, no anything but to sit & wait the coming of future events, & they all seem dark . . . with no look into the future except at the close, when my boys shall come again when God shall send them to bring their mother home & that home will never be desolate. . . .
>
> My tender gentle delicate babe was not meant to bear the burden & heat of the day, not meant to fight lifes battles, his merry heart for he was always laughing, always happy, but it was of his own kind; the toys & joys of children were not his; he was just happy to be let alone, happy because so pure, & because his fortune was, & is, bright. I often used to say & feel "why my child is different from other children, he doesn't seem to care for any body or anything." He looked as if all his pleasures were too lofty for communion here. We could not appreciate them.
>
> In Pa's birthday verse to me with a slight alteration I find some description of what seemed to be the measure of his namesakes joys & hopes. "This world's too small his hopes to measure, Above beyond the upper skies, Our gifted child has

Ella's letter to her parents after the death of her fourteen-month-old son, David.

found his treasure. And of all our bright & holy & high aspi-
rations for his coming greatness, none were so high as those
of his creator. . . . For of such is the kingdom of heaven."

And it is with . . . the deepest humility & gratitude that
I try and determine, to accept the offer of a home above,
among these sinless ones of earth. . . . His last knowing
look on earth was at me, just as the convulsion came on &
then, & then, his eyes fixed on heaven & they never changed
till "God finally touched him & he slept." Oh this long, long
weary night, when will morning come?

Fortunately Ella was not alone during the day while Genl was at the
post office or at his law office. Maggie and Lula, now four, arrived to
stay in Freeport, taking Ella to church and to visit neighbors. Yet, life
was difficult. In particular, she expressed sorrow to her father for the
loss of his namesake:

The most painful of all my duties, my dear Pa, is this of
writing letters home for stories of a mother's pride & love in
regard to the brightest dream of my life are the only thoughts
which present themselves & these thoughts I dare not think
for then I've no power or control such a long weary yearning
comes over me to go to my child, that it does seem as if the
slender chords of reason & the more slender chords of my life
must break & launch my boat on the silent sea which divides
me from him & Heaven both, with hopeful excellent joy that
I make in preparation for the journey so that David shall not
be disappointed when he comes down to the river to meet me
that he shall find his mother worthy of her son. . . .

> Say to my ma that since I left her, I've kept every promise in regard to our boy. I was good to him. No child was ever better loved.

If this despair were not enough, Ella also had to deal with Maggie's unhappiness in her marriage to Bunkey and with life in Illinois. Ella wrote that her sister-in-law was "not pleased here & I've never seen her pleased anywhere & if she complained now & I with great sorrow & surprise I admit she does, I don't know when she will be content. . . . I spent a few days with them. . . . He was busy night & day & kind, forbearing & patient under all circumstances. More than once I thanked God out of the fullness of my heart for the blessing of a brother." Ella hoped "for her sake & Bunk's that time will change her feelings & she may help him make his home a bright one."

Whatever the cause of Bunkey and Maggie's marital problems, Ella could not solve them, nor did she have the energy to do so. After David's death, she relied on Genl for emotional support. She wrote her mother on August 23, 1868, her third wedding anniversary:

> To my husband I turn & find there no change, just the same noble, best-loved & loving husband & in humility I thank God for this his greatest gift, always on the watch to find some stray beam to lighten my mournful pathway. . . . He is so good, so liberal, so kind.

But Ella's "mournful pathway" was about to grow longer.

* * * * *

IN MID-AUGUST, ELLA AND GENL received word from Chapel Hill that her father had been seriously injured in a fall from his carriage. They were assured that the prognosis was good and that sixty-seven-year-old President Swain would recover.

It had been a long summer in Chapel Hill. Losing their grandson had deeply affected the Swains. Further compounding their lives was the havoc being wrought by political tumult, which threatened their very future.

For more than three decades, David Swain had made the state of the university his primary concern. Mrs. Spencer wrote in her 1870 memoir:

> During the war, all his energies were exerted to preserve the University. . . . Immediately after the surrender, he visited Washington City, as one of the Delegates sent from North Carolina to confer with President Johnson on the forma- tion of a Provisional Government for the State. . . . After the establishment of Peace, Gov. Swain devoted himself with renewed energy to the restoration of the University to its former pride of place in the affections of our people.

Those first years of Reconstruction were difficult, Mrs. Spencer wrote, for "the ground swell that succeeded the storm was too heavy. Southern people were too much prostrated, and the spirit of the political parties sprang up, too bitter." Swain "struggled on . . . perseveringly . . . with the hope of interesting Northern capitalists in the financial condition of the University. . . . [With] great influence, he secured to North Carolina the Landscript donation from Congress for the establishment of an Agricultural school," one that in 1889 finally would open its doors as North Carolina College of Agriculture and Mechanic Arts (known today as North Carolina State University) in the state capital.

Swain was encountering new obstacles, however. All the university's endowment placed in Confederate bonds was lost, its property was mortgaged and carried a burdensome debt, and tuition generated from the fall enrollment of thirteen freshmen would not cover faculty salaries.

Although President Swain had offered to resign in July 1867, the trustees had not taken action, and classes went on as usual. But the new state constitution adopted in March 1868 gave the state Board of Education—and ultimately the governor—responsibility for appointing the university's board of trustees.

Of seventy-eight trustees, the governor reappointed only four. David Swain, who had served as a trustee since 1831, was not reappointed.

Despite the constantly shifting political landscape, President Swain never lost hope that his beloved university would succeed. But the pressures were taking their toll. By summer 1868, Mrs. Spencer noted, Swain "seemed suddenly . . . to droop and grow old, losing the vivacity and elasticity which had always distinguished him."

On July 23, the new board of trustees accepted the year-old offer of Swain and the entire faculty to resign. Without a president or faculty, the trustees "forcibly closed" the university.

Swain vehemently protested his dismissal. He argued that the university had been exceedingly successful under his tenure and that the state Charter of 1789 gave trustees power to remove the president only for "misbehavior, inability or neglect of duty," none of which pertained to his situation.

His efforts were for naught. The trustees thanked him for his service and declined to reverse their actions.

On the afternoon of August 11, a week after the university closed, President Swain and his friend Professor Manuel Fetter rode into the countryside to inspect a farm called Babylon that Swain had purchased in a mortgage default. Professor Fetter drove the buggy, pulled by a horse many believed to have been the very one General Sherman had given Swain three years earlier. During the ride, the horse turned abruptly, upsetting the buggy and throwing both men to the ground.

President Swain was carried across the campus on a stretcher and put to bed. At first, said his friend and Presbyterian minister, Professor Charles Phillips, he "did not strengthen or rally at all, though his mind was cheerful and sustained, his appetite was good and he could move himself with more freedom in the bed."

No one believed that his life was in danger. "After a week or two, he appeared to be in a fair way of recovery," getting in and out of bed, Mrs. Spencer reported. His progress may have accounted for Mrs. Swain's light correspondence to her daughter. She hadn't even sent word of the accident until a week after it happened.

Ella chided her mother for not keeping her informed:

> I have been breathless for the past three days waiting to hear from home. Mr. Emery's [Chapel Hill physician Thomas R. Emery] letter shocked me so. . . . It assumed that very bond on earth was to be severed at once. . . . Considering that two weeks had passed since the accident & we had not been informed by you that Pa must be very much better or not so badly injured as Mr. E's letter would indicate. . . . It is sufficient for me to know & to suffer that my own dear Pa is in pain & so far away that it is not in my power to be with & help you take care of him. . . . but if there was the slightest danger you surely would let us know.

She encouraged her mother to rely on "telegraphs & rail roads. . . . Pray don't lose time to make use of them."

Charles Phillips later wrote in *The North Carolina Presbyterian:*

> The injuries that he received were soon found to be superficial. But the shock that his nervous system sustained prevented a proper reaction from supervening. . . . On Wednesday he was very sanguine that he would soon be able to help himself in all his wants.

After the accident, President Swain no longer could visit and pray at Anne's grave in the backyard garden, as had been his daily custom. Instead, on Wednesday evening, August 26, "he went over the Lord's Prayer . . . [and] talked to Eleanor . . . of the 'communion of saints' and his enjoyment of the ideas and prospect the expression conceived."

The next morning, Phillips reported:

> I found him sitting up for the first time and learned that he had been doing so for about an hour. I congratulated him on the success of this new effort, and expressed the hope that he would be walking about in a few days.
>
> He thanked me and made some reference to a historic matter we had been discussing the night before. Presently he asked to be helped back to bed. When placed in his usual position, he seemed to be very much exhausted and gasped for breath, the family physician was sent for and with the neighbors responded quickly to his room to offer him assistance.
>
> But all the effort of love and friendship, guided by professional skills, were in vain: Gov. Swain died in some 20 minutes after he returned to bed.
>
> I do not think that he was aware of his danger. Nor did his attendants (his wife, his nurse, and Prof. Phillips) feel

alarmed until the cold sweat broke out and he became pale. The only words that he spoke (which I remember) after he lay down were "give me something to drink"—"I am very weak"—"raise me up"—"lay me down."

Six days after Ella had written her mother, begging to be kept better informed, she and Genl, accompanied by Bunkey, Maggie, and Lula, set out on the long journey to Chapel Hill. The *Freeport Journal* reported, "Gen. Atkins received a telegram from Raleigh, North Carolina, conveying to him the sad news of the death of his father-in-law. . . . In their sudden bereavement the family have the sympathy of their many friends in this section of the country."

The obituary Mrs. Spencer wrote for her long-time friend must have provided some comfort to Ella:

> Gov. Swain's faith was firm, and his eyes undimmed, as he looked forward to crossing the river. That night before his death (in no apprehension of what was to happen in the morrow), he spoke of a conversation he had held some years ago with the late Dr. James Phillips, on the foundation of the Christian's hope; and giving his old friend's clear, condensed declaration of faith in Jesus Christ's atoning work as the only sure ground or hope in death, he added that it had been a great comfort to him ever since. . . . Dr. Phillips, he said, and himself were both moved to tears as they talked.

Mrs. Spencer believed President Swain's "work was done, and well done, and he could safely leave his reputation to his fellow countrymen, and to future times." Years later she wrote to Mrs. Swain:

When August comes in I always think more than usual of you. . . . On the 27th he left these scenes of his labors on earth for higher employments & pleasures.

In another letter to Mrs. Swain, she noted:

I have been thinking of you, & of what happened over yonder in your old home to-day fourteen years ago. . . . What horror & dismay for all of us. . . . What years of trouble, anxiety, mortification, impotent rage & vexation, long protracted & well-nigh hopeless waiting were then entered upon by all who loved him & loved the University.

That "hopeless waiting" is what truly caused his death, wrote *Raleigh State Chronicle* editor Josephus Daniels during the university's 1889 Centennial celebration:

President Swain died of a broken heart. . . . His injuries were considered slight, but his spirit was broken and he had neither hope nor power to rally. He could not survive the death of what was to him the dearest object on earth.

Following the August 29 funeral at the President's House, David Lowry Swain was buried in the backyard garden beside his daughters, Anne and "Infant Ella," and his son David. As Mrs. Spencer later recalled, many gatherings had taken place over the years in the family's "ample and beautiful yard"—from commencement dinners to receptions for U.S. Presidents—James K. Polk in 1847, James Buchanan in 1859, and Andrew Johnson in 1867. But not until President Swain's funeral had there ever been "an assemblage . . . in Chapel Hill of more general or deeper or sadder interest than met . . . to pay the last honors to him who has so long been the center of Chapel Hill life. Every class of the citizens of Chapel Hill was represented—through the wide piazzas or standing in the yard under the shadow of the oak trees."

CHAPTER 10

Moving On

AFTER PRESIDENT SWAIN'S funeral, Ella and Genl remained in Chapel Hill to help Mrs. Swain, while Bunkey and his family returned to Illinois. When the Atkinses arrived home in Freeport a few weeks later, they discovered that Maggie was very ill.

Ella wrote her mother that Maggie was in bed, "very much emaciated and very feeble and very low spirited, but our arrival so cheered her up that she could sit up and walk across the floor before I left her. . . . One side from her shoulder to her foot is a good deal paralyzed and it will at best be a long time before she can entirely recover if she ever does."

Expressing bewilderment at her family's many tragedies, Ella wrote Mrs. Swain:

> How strange it seems the events of this changing life. It seems impossible for me to realize the scene through which I've passed in the last few months. It is a mercy to us that God throws a drapery around these heavy burdens which so shrouds the strength of the stern reality & enables us to survive the sorrow which, if we did fully comprehend, would smite us to the earth.

When Mrs. Swain did not respond immediately, Ella complained, "We had waited without hearing a word . . . a full month." She worried about her, noting, "Often how I wish I were with you my own Mamy that we might talk over the turns of the past sad years. I don't feel satisfied to write. I want to talk it all over with you & it seems as if the burden would not then be so heavy."

Eventually some semblance of a daily routine resumed in the Atkins household. With Ella nursing her, Maggie slowly recovered. But Ella did not feel settled: "Genl has been going the rounds of speaking & I've been with him on one or two campaigns & out to Shannon," she wrote her mother. "[It] is so dark at home when he my only light is gone."

Little David was always in her thoughts.

On her twenty-sixth birthday, Ella returned from visiting Maggie and Lula, bringing back a turkey, "my birthday present from Bunkey." That morning, her husband had left "an elegant gold watch" by her dinner place. She wrote her mother, "Don't you think I fared well, my Mamy?"

Over the years, Genl had been unfailingly generous, giving her jewelry and books, including a small volume of Robert Burns's poetry with a card that read:

> These poems of Burns were presented to me by your father, before our marriage. At first, they were bound in paper. Some years after, he had them rebound as you see. Keep them for his and my sake. "The Cotter's Saturday Night" was your pa's favorite. All of it was mine, as he gave it to me. How careful was he of his books.

On the back inside cover was the notation in Mrs. Swain's handwriting, *given Eleanor H. White by David L. Swain—3 years afterwards 'Mr. & Mrs. Swain,' The Cotter of Saturday night—his favorite*:

> . . . O Thou! who pour'd the patriotic tide,
> That stream'd thro' Wallace's undaunted heart,
> Who dar'd to nobly stem tyrannic pride,
> Or nobly die, the second glorious part:
> (The patriot's God peculiarly thou art,
> His friend, inspirer, guardian, and reward!) . . .

Burns's words may have resonated differently for the couple. For Ella, it perhaps reminded her of her father, his love of country and acquiescence to secession only when he felt he had no choice. For Genl, it may have spoken to his resolve to fight to keep his country united and of his ancestors' sacrifice in fighting for America's independence. Together, they may have read something of their own courageous love story in the Burns poem.

But no amount of celebration could distract her from the events of the past few years. She wrote her mother:

> If it were not for the bitter vissons [*sic*] which I cannot forget
> under any circumstances. I should be very happy, but my
> heart longs for focus from voices forever gone from earth . . .
> looking over those times given me with eyes full of tears by
> that best of God anointed, my father now in heaven.

She missed "the bright babe which was our comfort," and looked to the day when "this little family on earth may be a family in Heaven"; she missed "in all the world my father."

Ella hoped that remembrances of her father would cheer her grieving mother:

> I find two lines & let them come to & comfort you now as if from his own lips. The verses are from a dying husband to his wife. . . . "Leona goodbye; should the grief that is gathering now, ever be too dark for your faith, you will long for relief and remember this journey tho lonesome is brief. Over low land and river to me". . . . I hope it will bring to you my poor suffering Mamy some little light in your darksome path.

Mrs. Swain finally wrote, but did not mention her latest difficulties: The UNC trustees had begun the process of appointing President Swain's successor. Although it would be January 1869 before the Reverend Solomon Pool would be named president, Mrs. Swain felt it necessary to leave the President's House and the town she had called home for decades.

In late 1868, she returned to Raleigh and White Hall, her childhood home, moving in with her sisters Emma and Susan White, and Betsy Felton, now widowed. Ella seemed supportive of this arrangement, writing a cheerful letter December 3 and inquiring about her aunts: "I send a kiss for each. . . . I love them . . . & each broken link in our family chain only serves to make those remaining doubly strong."

She was relieved that her mother's transition from Chapel Hill to Raleigh had been relatively smooth. But she never failed to let Mrs. Swain know how much she missed her: "When I see other ladies with their mothers visiting them I long for my mamy too oh I do wish you were here."

Leaving Chapel Hill also meant moving the family graves from the President's House backyard. Buried there were Mrs. Swain's husband, her son David, and her daughters Anne and "Infant" Ella, as well as Bunkey's first wife, Susan.

It took more than a year to reinter her loved ones. She purchased a shaded site in Raleigh's new Oakwood Cemetery and selected a marble obelisk to mark the Swains' final resting place. When that day finally came to move the graves, Mrs. Spencer expressed outrage that the caskets, exhumed from the President's House yard, had been stored overnight in President Pool's barn, when several vacant university offices would have made a more respectful holding room.

* * * * *

AS COMFORTING AS SHE tried to be to her mother, Ella still felt melancholy. Nonetheless, she was dutiful as ever, continuing to do all that was expected of her:

> Sat. week ago, I had several of my neighbors to tea with me & on Monday morning . . . I spent the day with Mag . . . & came home, bringing Mag & Lula with us. Mag left us the next afternoon & came in again on Friday morning & remained till Monday afternoon. . . . Thanksgiving, Genl & I went to church in the forenoon & dined at Mr. Barretts at 4 in the afternoon. & on Friday I had all of Genls family that could come to dine. . . . You see my dear Ma, I've been very much employed for this past week.

In December, Genl took Ella to Chicago, though friends with whom they were to travel canceled at the last minute. She wrote her mother from the city that her husband always had her best interests at heart: "My good, kind, thoughtful husband, knowing . . . I was not very well, decided not to disappoint his wife on the visit. . . . I am feeling much better & we go home this evening. I had probably over-taxed my strength & caused my indisposition during the past few days."

Rest was necessary because Ella was four months pregnant. But their always-busy lives did not let up, especially when Atkins entered into a new business venture, an insurance agency, with his brother-in-law, Martin Krinbill.

Hoping to cheer her mother, Ella described a supper party for her neighbors, complete with dishes made from her North Carolina recipes: turkey and lobster salad, scalloped and fried oysters, "your kind of muffins . . . your risen cake, coconut pudding and pineapple gin and coffee." She ended her newsy letter, "I write you all my house hold odds & ends because you are my mamy & I know will be interested in every thing about your child & it will at last serve to pass by one of the moments which make life."

Ella was ready for the year to end, however, dubbing 1868 the "bitter weary sad darkest year of my life."

* * * * *

WITH A NEW YEAR came a renewed focus on the project General Atkins had long hoped to see completed: the Soldiers' Monument "to the memory of our dead heroes who are buried away from home." Chairing the project, Atkins called for the entire community to raise funds. He spoke of similar committees throughout the South, gathering up

> from the battle-fields the rebel dead, and bury[ing] them again in cemeteries set apart for that purpose. . . . On the first of May . . . each year, those burial places are clothed in evergreens and smothered in flowers. . . . If the Southern people still cherish the memories of their rebel dead . . . who went down to their graves in defeat, how much more should the people of the Northland cherish the memory of their dead heroes, whose graves are victory crowned.

His proposed design for the monument was approved in early 1869; ten months later, the cornerstone was laid in an elaborate ceremony. The event featured a formal procession attracting "a large crowd of citizens, both of the city and county . . . and Stephenson street was lined with spectators," reported the *Freeport Journal*. Atkins gave an "eloquent address. . . . Everything passed off harmoniously." A time capsule was placed. It contained a copy of the U.S. Constitution, a list of soldiers who had died, revenue stamps, currency, copies of local newspapers, and Masonic meeting proceedings.

* * * * *

ELLA SPENT EARLY 1869 in confinement, awaiting the
arrival of a new baby. On May 31, at nine o'clock in the evening, the Atkinses welcomed their first daughter, Eleanor
Hope Atkins. Genl said she was no bigger than a dot, so Dot became
her name.

Now a mother for the third time, Ella had plenty of help with baby
Dot. On hand were her sister-in-law Maggie and niece Lula, as well as
nurse Ellen Emmer and servant Jennie Maggins.

Their emotional support was important when the general's seventy-
nine-year-old father, Adna, died on August 6. The *Freeport Journal's*
obituary revealed some of the long-time resident's early adventures and
later contributions:

> Adna S. Atkins was apprenticed to learn the tailoring trade
> . . . in Philadelphia. Being naturally of a roving disposition,
> he started out on an extended tour of observation at the con-
> clusion of his apprenticeship, and spent several years abroad
> wandering through France, England and Scotland. . . .
> Of his five sons, four enlisted in the army and battled for
> the cause which their father and their grandfather had so
> chorused and so nobly promoted and *preserved.* . . . Mr. Atkins
> was a member of the Masonic Fraternity for upwards of fifty
> years, being one of the oldest Masons in the county. . . .

Four months later, Sarah Atkins also died. This was the woman
who Smith Atkins once had declared "always makes better mush and
bakes better bread and churns butter better than anybody else." The

newspaper reported, "For upward of half a century, Mrs. Atkins had been a consistent member of the Methodist Episcopal Church, and died in full confidence of a blessed immortality."

To cope with his grief, Atkins stayed busy. His legal business was brisk. He was organizing the five-year reunion of the Ninety-second Illinois. And, he joined forces with Congressman H.C. Burchard, owner of the *Freeport Journal*, to run that paper.

Ella, on the other hand, missed the South. Mrs. Swain traveled to Freeport for granddaughter Dot's first birthday. But when the family took Mrs. Swain home in late August, Ella and Dot remained in Raleigh while Genl returned to Freeport.

He visited Raleigh over Christmas, and refuted a December 27 report, printed in the competing *Freeport Bulletin*, that "Gen. Atkins and family arrived home on Saturday last from the Sunny South." He offered his own version of events:

> We wish the *Bulletin* was right about it; unfortunately for us our "better half," with little "Dot," still remain in that "far off Sunny Southern Clime," and we are alone, with the mercury down to ten degrees below zero; ugh! whew!

When Genl finally brought his family back to Freeport, it was fall of 1871. Mrs. Swain came with them. Governor Graham informed his wife he had seen Susan and Emma White in December, and "Mrs. Swain will not return probably this winter." She decided to brave the Freeport winter because Ella was pregnant. Mrs. Spencer wrote Mrs. Swain of "Ella's prospects . . . as among the strong reasons for you delaying to return home. I wish her well through her trial—poor girl! I dare say you suffer as much in anticipation for her as she does. I was glad for both your sakes you can be with her."

* * * * *

ALTHOUGH NEVER a regular churchgoer, Mrs. Swain placed great importance on religion. Years earlier, she had written her friend Selina Wheat that Ella "professed religion," and she hoped that her daughter would learn to rely on "his help."

Faith had been an important part of Ella's upbringing. Letters from her aunts were filled with directives to include prayer and belief in God in her daily life. At home, the Swains read the New Testament together, copying inspirational messages in its front and back covers.

Instinctively, the Atkinses relied on their faith to help them through the loss of sons Graham and David, as well as Ella's sister and father, and Genl's parents. But the family's faith was tested yet again on January 29, 1872, when Bunkey was killed in a freak accident while boarding a train.

His death was particularly devastating to Ella, who believed Bunkey had finally found his calling as a compassionate physician and trusted community member. "My brother is poor," she had written her mother when he opened his practice in Shannon. "But for the first time in his life a Man & worthy of every assistance & encouragement his friends can give."

The *Freeport Journal* remembered "Richard Caswell Swain, M.D." as a person of "buoyant spirits and kindly sympathy" and with "noble impulses" and "warm-hearted generosity." No one, it was reported, "had more friends or warmer ones." He would be "mourned by a wide circle of friends and acquaintances . . . not the least . . . will be the poor and unfortunate, who were always certain of his generous sympathy, and frequently of his bounty."

Bunkey Swain shortly after he began his medical practice in Illinois.

His North Carolina friends expressed sorrow. Professor Charles Phillips wrote Mrs. Swain that he had learned of the death when he received copies of the *Freeport Journal,* confirming "a report which greatly distressed me—that your son—your only son had been cut off from the land of the living in the prime of his life. . . ." He acknowledged Bunkey's importance to Mrs. Swain: "The obituary tells some of the reasons why Richard's friends should mourn his untimely death. But none of them were peculiar to a mother. Her heart knows its bitterness and knows it alone."

A former Swain servant, then living with the Phillips family, said, "It might true that the poor would miss Marse Richard."

Mrs. Spencer wrote of a friend who "wept abundantly when talking of Richard. He had not an enemy in the world—& as his obituary truly said, the poor would be among his chief mourners." She expressed relief that Mrs. Swain was with Ella in Illinois, for "her affection, & devotion to you will do more for you than the sympathy of all other friends united. . . ."

Though Mrs. Spencer expected Eleanor Swain to return to Raleigh with Bunkey's remains "to rest among his kindred," he was buried in Freeport. It was winter, and her former neighbor speculated, "Severe weather still detains you."

Also keeping her in Illinois was Ella, who had been unwell and perhaps had suffered a miscarriage shortly after Bunkey's death. By spring, when Mrs. Swain might have returned home, Ella discovered she was again pregnant. Mrs. Swain decided to remain in Freeport.

A year that had begun with devastating loss ended with hope restored when her new grandson, Smith Dykins ("Dyke"), was born on November 30, 1872.

Meanwhile, the newly widowed Maggie left Illinois. She and Lula, now eight, returned to Shelbyville to live with her widowed mother.

Eventually, Maggie remarried, this time to a distant cousin, Bailey Peyton (Dick) Steele, and had two more daughters. No extant letters mention visits between the former in-laws and cousins, but photographs of them altogether show they stayed in touch.

* * * * *

As the writings of Mrs. Spencer and Smith Atkins mentioned, Freeport winters were notoriously severe. Accompanied by bitter temperatures and wind, snow often covered the ground by Thanksgiving and remained until April. Early in her marriage, Ella had written her father, "This memorable month of March . . . comes in today with snow sleet and the lion in his most furious form for all day long the wind has roared most savagely."

As a young man, Smith Atkins described the town's wintry conditions in his journal:

> Today we have mail for the first time in a long while. This snowstorm the most severe of any within my recollection has almost entirely cut us off from any communications with the world without. It is so badly drifted that the railroads are completely blockaded and it is said that there are drifts on the Rock Island road 40 feet deep.

Just as her mother had a generation earlier, Ella yearned for the milder winters of the North Carolina Piedmont. She decided to take her children south each winter to stay at White Hall, an arrangement that provided comfort for both daughter and mother.

Ella and her children had already arrived for their usual stay in Raleigh in 1874 when she gave birth to Richard Swain Atkins on October 9. Named for his late uncle, baby Richard was much doted upon by his mother and grandmother.

* * * * *

WITH HIS FAMILY IN THE SOUTH, General Atkins helped write *Ninety-Second Illinois Volunteers,* a memoir published in spring of 1875. In addition to his professional duties, he continued to lead an active community life. But his family's arrival back in Freeport for the summer may have precipitated his decision to sell his interest in the *Freeport Journal.* Having one less business obligation would give him more time to spend with Ella and their three children, as well as to focus on his many volunteer activities.

No sooner had he shed that enormous responsibility than he and Ella once again experienced tragedy. On September 16, 1875, three weeks before his first birthday, Richard died. As with David's death seven years earlier, the cause of death was not known. The date was dutifully recorded in the family Bible.

Richard's death affected Ella differently than had those of Graham and David. As always, she was grateful for her husband's loving support. Mrs. Swain was also there to offer comfort. Mother, like daughter, had lost three young children—David died a week after his first birthday; David Swain Jr. died two months before his sixth birthday; and "Infant Ella," born on the Swains' sixteenth wedding anniversary (January 12, 1842), died ten months later.

When "Infant Ella" died, just weeks before the birth of another daughter she would name Ella, Mrs. Swain had Anne and Bunkey to care for. Now the second daughter she had named Ella had two children of her own who needed their mother's attention.

CHAPTER 11

Ella

THE RHYTHM OF THEIR LIVES continued—Ella and the children lived with Mrs. Swain in Raleigh during the fall and winter. Genl traveled to Raleigh late each spring to bring everyone back to Freeport for the summer.

All the while, Mrs. Spencer kept them informed of happenings in Chapel Hill. "I have lived to see another Commencement," she wrote Ella in June 1876. "Have lived to see the Chapel crowded once more." (After having been closed for five years, the university reopened in the fall of 1875 with about one hundred students.)

Her one disappointment with commencement, she told Mrs. Swain later that summer, was that former Governor Vance had not been there to deliver a eulogy of President Swain, eight years after his death. Mrs. Spencer wanted everyone attending "to hear justice done" to her old friend "by one who knew him well, and owed so much to him!"

(Vance's son, David, had been expelled from the university in spring 1876 for behavior problems; his father "could not get over it," Mrs. Spencer wrote. "I was disappointed in [the governor] that he showed so little self-control.")

A year later, certain the university was back on sure footing, she expressed hope that "Ella means to send her oldest son" to the University of North Carolina.

Whether David Swain's grandson, Dyke, would enroll was a decision that was years away. He was three years old when Mrs. Spencer expressed that hope. He and his sister, Dot, were at White Hall with their mother that winter when their new baby sister, Susan Annie, was born on December 10, 1877. Named in honor of Ella's aunt and in memory of her sister, the baby had light blonde hair and a heart-shaped face, her father's eyes, and her mother's nose and lips. She was called Susie.

Life at White Hall with Ella's three children was busy. Three generations, including great-aunts, kept the days full. Mrs. Spencer wrote in March that she hoped Ella and "her children are well & strong." In fact, when the general arrived in Raleigh that spring to bring them home, he found them thriving.

A good and loving mother, Ella was in her element. The flyleaf of an 1859 edition of *The Ice King and the Sweet South Wind* was inscribed years later by Dot: *This book was Eleanor Hope Swain's—Eleanor Hope Atkins loved to hear her mother read it—she read it to her daughter Eleanor Hope Atkins Cobb.*

A windowpane at White Hall revealed the close bond between mother and daughter: Scratched in the glass was the name *Ella* and, below it, *Dot Atkins.* Ella and her oldest child had shared what surely was a moment of delight—etching their names on glass.

MCHENRY.   Freeport

Ella in 1880, wearing a locket her husband had given her, engraved with *Eleanor H. Atkins.*

* * * * *

Y EAR IN AND YEAR OUT, Ella and the Atkins children continued to divide their time between the North and the South. Spring 1881 didn't seem different from any other in North Carolina's capital. Ella and her young children were once again at White Hall with Mrs. Swain and her sisters. But instead of returning to Illinois as the weather grew warmer, Ella decided to extend their stay in North Carolina.

She corresponded regularly with Genl, keeping him apprised of their daily life.

Suddenly, everything changed. On Saturday, June 11, he received a letter from Ella mentioning that several members of Mrs. Swain's household were sick with influenza. She assured her husband that she and the children were well.

Over the next few days, Ella nursed those who had been stricken. By Monday, she too was sick.

In Freeport, Atkins had just finished dinner Monday evening, when he received a dispatch informing him that Ella was "dangerously ill." Desperate to be with her, he immediately made the necessary travel arrangements. But before he could pack his suitcase, another telegram arrived.

* * * * *

T HE NEWS WAS UNFATHOMABLE: Ella was dead. The *Freeport Bulletin* reported, "The uncertainty of human life in this world has been again made manifest by the sudden taking off at her childhood home in Raleigh, North Carolina, of the wife of our respected and honored citizen, Gen. Smith D. Atkins. . . . [It was] so unexpected, so sudden, that it came like a hard blow to the bereaved husband and father, who worshipped his wife and children."

Atkins left Freeport "on the midnight train to attend the last sad rites." But with such a long distance to travel, he did not arrive in Raleigh in time for Ella's funeral, which took place three days after her death.

Memorialized in a simple service at home, Ella was buried at Oakwood Cemetery beside her beloved father and sister who had been reinterred there in 1869.

Her tombstone simply read, *Wife of Smith Dykins Atkins.*

Revealing how attitudes toward the North-South union had been tempered over the years, Ella's obituary in the *Raleigh Register* referred to her husband, the once-controversial General Smith Dykins Atkins, as

> an officer of prominence in the Federal Army, who met and married her soon after the war, at her home in Chapel Hill. . . . [Ella] was an estimable lady, held in much esteem by a large number of friends both here and at her home in Freeport, Ill.

At thirty-eight, Ella Atkins, mother, wife, and daughter, was "a lady endowed with rare intellect, and had a large circle of friends in this city who regret her demise," reported the *Freeport Bulletin*.

She had been an affectionate and doting mother to her six children, three of whom—Dot, twelve; Dyke, nine; and Susie, three-and-a-half—survived her and would never forget her.

As a friend, Ella had been dedicated and generous: "I've been very much employed for this past week," she once wrote, "so much company dear Ma & the company I felt in duty bound to have for I am so much in debt to all my friends."

She had difficulty finishing a November 1868 letter home, as "one thing & then another among them was to prepare for & entertain 11 of my neighbors who took tea with me last evening." She once apologized for not writing a longer letter, explaining, "company this week & a number of calls to return" would keep her "quite busy."

As a sister, daughter, sister-in-law, and aunt, Ella was devoted. On the first anniversary of her sister Anne's death, she wrote:

> This month dear Ma is filled with sad recollections & no one I reckon dwells on them more than you & I. These last sad days one year ago, these closing hours of that dear life on earth & the dawning of a new & bright one.

Before Maggie and Lula moved to Illinois, Ella always remembered them in letters home: "give my love & the photo marked for her to Mag. . . . tell little Lula Uncle & Auntie often talk about her & send her a whole heap of kisses." She was proud of her brother who had overcome adversity. Ella boasted that Genl's "entire family think every thing of Bunk & oh I am so pleased to tell you that we hear the very best accounts. . . . Bunkey is busy all the while."

Ella believed Southern ill-will toward her marriage had faded, commenting in March 1868 how "during my last stay in Chapel Hill I won't forget their [Judge Battle, Professor Phillips, and their wives] kindness, nor do I forget the cherished friends of my sister."

Upon learning of Ella's death, Professor Charles Phillips sent words of condolence to his friend Mrs. Swain, just as he had when Bunkey died:

> As soon as we heard of this new sorrow which our Father in Heaven has sent on you—I was moved to write and assure you of our sympathy with you. It is all that we mortals can do for each other when heart and flesh fail.
>
> We have prayed for you that in this your day of darkness light may give you a silver linning [*sic*] to this black cloud. Such is our prayer at our family devotions and such it will be. . . . I and my wife hope that you will think of us as frequently thinking of you and as desirous of lessening your sorrow in any way that we can.

Mrs. Swain now had lost her husband and all her children. Mrs. Spencer commiserated:

> You sit a childless widow. I do not know how you have lived through this summer! If we did not know that God is good we would say of such afflictions as you have borne that they were cruel.
>
> There have been few days for two months past that I have not thought of Ella—recalled her childhood, her girlhood, her marriage. Brother Sam . . . saw her in Raleigh last Novr: "most cordial, agreeable, and comely." . . . I can see Ella, as I write. . . . I hope her daughter, Dot, looks like her.

General Atkins had lost his love—the feisty young woman who had taunted him about the clumsiness of his first acrostic. Their love story had been one of the most controversial in mid-nineteenth century North Carolina. Yet they never doubted their love for one another.

Ella had once assured her mother:

> . . . to me he is my lifes [*sic*] greatest blessing my noble gener-ous husband. . . . To Genl Atkins my husband I am most indebted than ever a woman would and I'm content with him any where on God's green earth, with the simple discharge of any duty he does his faithfully & has ever been all this world to me.

CHAPTER 12

Legacies

A
FTER ELLA'S DEATH, the bond between Mrs. Swain and her son-in-law, Smith Atkins, grew ever stronger. Having outlived her children, Mrs. Swain did not want to lose her grandchildren to Illinois. She "begged the general not to take the children back to Freeport with him," wrote Mrs. Swain's great-great-granddaughter "Wuff" Newell, "but to let them live with her. General Atkins . . . granted her request." Dot, Dyke, and Susie remained with their grandmother through fall and winter of 1881.

During the school year, Dot attended St. Mary's, her mother's alma mater, "where it was hoped the companionship of girls her age would help her forget her recent sadness," Newell explained.

Their father visited at least once, at Christmas, when the family posed for a photograph. It shows them dressed in mourning clothes, their expressions melancholy.

As he had for many years, Atkins traveled to Raleigh in the spring of 1882, but again left the children with Mrs. Swain when he returned to Freeport. Mrs. Spencer wrote her on August 27, "I suppose you have been enjoying Dot's company all the [school] vacation."

Their presence also helped Mrs. Swain cope with the deaths of her sisters Emma and Susan that fall. She had shared White Hall with them for fourteen years since David Swain's death.

With her grandchildren there to brighten her spirits, Mrs. Swain turned her attention to a controversy that had plagued her for years: the ownership of her husband's collection of papers.

As a young man, David Swain had been interested in documenting North Carolina history. In 1833, he helped to establish the North Carolina Historical Society to collect and preserve the state's public records. Although the state General Assembly supported its incorporation and purpose, the organization was never active. In 1844, it was superseded by the Historical Society of the University of North Carolina, dedicated to recording the state's colonial government and role in the American Revolution.

Voted its president, Swain contributed many works he had acquired to the new organization, which was active only during commencement each year when an historical address was given. Nevertheless, Swain continued to gather documents.

In 1868, as Mrs. Swain prepared to move out of the President's House in Chapel Hill, she packed up her husband's papers and books along with other family belongings. She considered the collection of historical documents—including letters written by her own grandfather, Richard Caswell, the state's first governor—to be part of her late husband's estate. The papers had not been mentioned in Swain's will; therefore she considered them to be legally hers. The university's new president and trustees made no claim otherwise.

She shipped her husband's papers to a Raleigh bank where they were stored in a vault. For years, the documents seemed all but forgotten by everyone except Mrs. Swain, who quietly guarded them.

Five years later, in 1873, Judge Battle asked to look through the documents. Mrs. Swain denied his request, writing that the collection had been the long-time "labor of my husband, a sacred trust, not to be intermeddled with, without the advice of some friend interested

Smith Atkins and his children in December 1881, six months after Ella's death.

& competent to decide for me." She did not say who that friend might be. She also promised to bequeath to the state or university those papers that Ella—David Swain's only surviving child—did not want to keep.

Historian H.G. Jones speculated that Mrs. Swain's response may have had more to do with the political climate than with her unwillingness to open the collection to Judge Battle. She and many prominent alumni believed the university libraries and archives had "fallen into the hands of vandals"—Reconstructionists.

Regardless of her reasons, she insisted that she was the rightful owner of the collection. Several of David Swain's colleagues argued otherwise, maintaining that the many historical documents and books had not been mentioned in his will because he knew they did not belong to him, but to the state. In fact, when Mrs. Swain later found proof that bound books belonged to the society, she quickly surrendered them.

In 1875, yet another historical society was incorporated, and a committee comprised of Mrs. Spencer and former governors Graham and Vance tried again to convince Mrs. Swain to give it her husband's collection. Mrs. Spencer made an "earnest request" of her friend to turn over "the collections of material of every kind, pertaining to the history of North Carolina, made by the late President Swain . . ." which could be "liable to damage from insects" if not properly preserved.

Perhaps preoccupied with Ella's growing family and life at White Hall, Mrs. Swain had no energy for debate: "I must decline to do so . . . I cannot indicate at this moment what disposition I will eventually make of that collection." Now in her seventies, she promised its contents would be "carefully preserved" and disposed of "in the future [to] most nearly comply with the intentions and desires of my late husband."

Graham, the society's president, believed Mrs. Swain had "made a mistake," declining their request because she erroneously viewed the historical society and the Reconstruction-era university trustees as being of "the same corporation," he wrote Mrs. Spencer.

He was correct. Mrs. Swain saw them both as "institutions of the state." As such, the society was as culpable as the university in betraying her husband by declining to pay back salary due him and maligning his tenure as president. Graham may have understood. He also had been slighted by Reconstruction leaders: After being elected to the U.S. Senate in 1865, Graham arrived in Washington, only to be denied his seat.

Yet, he argued, how could Mrs. Swain consider "the Historical matter . . . which was so freely yielded to him [David Swain]" as individual property? The issue created a rift between the long-time friends and remained unresolved when Governor Graham died two months later.

After Graham's death, the society elected a new president: William Hooper, a former antagonist of David Swain. Many years earlier, when Swain had been named university president, Hooper remarked that "the people of North Carolina have given Governor Swain all the offices they have to bestow and now have sent him to the university to be educated."

Mrs. Swain asked that all further correspondence on the subject of her husband's papers be directed to Ella.

Pressure began anew in summer 1876. Judge Battle produced a paper "showing that Gov. Swain held these documents as Trustee." Also, publicity about the controversy was causing people who had donated documents to Swain to attempt to reclaim them.

Mrs. Spencer urged Mrs. Swain to change her mind. If the collection were given to the historical society, she reasoned, donors would rescind their claims.

Mrs. Swain did not budge.

* * * *

WHETHER ELLA or General Atkins carried on negotiations with the society isn't known. With a growing family, Ella would have had little time to address such matters. Atkins, too, would have been hard-pressed to take up the fight. In addition to family, professional, and community responsibilities, he became politically active in the late 1870s.

A Republican Party loyalist, Atkins had run unsuccessfully for the U.S. Senate in 1870. Even he was surprised six years later when the Chicago *Evening Journal* suggested, "Gen. Smith D. Atkins, of Freeport, for Congress in the Fifth District wouldn't be bad."

The call to elective office was followed by a lighthearted response from the editors of the *Freeport Journal:*

> If the District was not now ably and acceptably represented in Congress [by H.C. Burchard, the *Journal*'s former owner], we would like to see General Atkins sent to Washington as a fitting off-set to some of the rebel Generals sent from the South. . . . [He] is one of the leading Republicans of this Congressional District, an able and eloquent political debater, with a record as a soldier, that has not a blot to mar it.

Since the Civil War, men who had once fought for the Confederacy and achieved the rank of colonels and generals had been elected to Congress. This rankled the Republican Party, which wanted its own former Union generals in Congress.

Atkins was perfect for the job, the *Evening Journal* proclaimed:

> As a soldier, he did not speculate in cotton or anything else, and came out of the war as poor as he went into it; and as a civilian office holder, before and since the war, not a dollar of public funds, beyond his legitimate salary, has ever stuck to his fingers.

The editors didn't mention that their candidate was a proponent of a united country, taking every opportunity to encourage healing the division between North and South. He told those gathered the following spring for Decoration Day in Rochelle, Illinois:

> As there came an end to the actual conflict, so there must come, sometime, an end to the estrangement and bitterness the conflict occasioned. We were brothers before the contest; it was a family quarrel; we are brothers now and brothers we must remain. . . . The wounds were deep, the scars are plain yet time will cover up the scars.

He often repeated the phrase, "We must not be enemies. We must be friends . . . I believe, I most earnestly hope, that the estrangements occasioned by the late war between the sections are gradually wearing away and dying out."

* * * * *

I N HIS OWN HOUSEHOLD, Atkins had witnessed the "wearing away and dying out" of estrangements. Mrs. Swain, the last in Ella's family to forgive and forget the Yankees, had grown attached to the general.

Ella had never stopped trying to bridge the gap between her mother and Atkins. Throughout her marriage, she filled her letters home with examples of her Genl's love and kindness. She ended them with "Genl joins me in love"; "Genl my good good man joins me in tenderest remembrances to my loved ones"; and "Genl joins in love sympathy & anxiety."

She found an ally in her brother. After Bunkey moved to Illinois, she wrote her parents of his admiration for General Atkins:

> He says that his success will be owing to Genl entirely that he was the very man in whose hands he should have fallen & his treatment of him has been very different from any he ever before received & said he "I tell you what Ella we should every one look on your marriage as a blessing for I tell you I would have been lost if I had not come under his care."

Occasionally she chided her mother for not responding to his letters: "Genl loves you too Ma & has written you several times since we left you. I wish you would write him as he is just as good to me as if I were his baby."

Despite her cool demeanor, Mrs. Swain, it seems, had grown fond of her son-in-law and, in some ways, even sooner than expected. A year after Ella and the general married, Mrs. Swain wrote a poem, "Tri-Coloured Flag," dedicated to her Yankee son-in-law:

I <u>must not</u> say I love thee, tri-coloured flag of old,

For thou has scoffed at our defeat & there's blood on every fold

I <u>will not</u> say I hate thee, proud banner of our foes—

For in childhood I did love thee, and that thy self dost know.

For four long years I've called thee a traitor to our land

Four long years of blood shed, thou didst all defiant stand

Yet again thou camest among us, shall I greet & call thee friend?

Ah! No old Flag, dark folds of crape with thy tri-colours blend.

Pale faces rise before me, from many a southern grave,

And midst these sad reflections I cannot bid thee wave

<u>Thou</u> has not shed our nations blood Ah well I grant that true

But strong men rushed to strike beneath thy folds, "red white & blue."

Thou didst not rob our southern land or burn our sunny home

Ah! No, not thou, & yet old Flag the Tyrant thou led'st on.

And yet old Flag I come not, with bitter taunt & jeer

To tell thus of thy treason, & ask how camest thou here.

As Peace the bright-eyed seraph, tho' stranger has spread her wing

O'er the golden shaft above thee, I can but listen to her sing,

* <u>Hope's</u> star is shining near thee, full of promise pure & bright,

Guiding forth this brave young warrior from his four long years of night.

And tho' thou hast acted treason, & scorned our "southern <u>rag</u>."

I will have to love & bless thee, & say "<u>my country's Flag</u>"!

Add another leaf of Laurel, to thy commanders crown.

And whisper to him softly, "<u>her colours are not Brown</u>."

At the end of the poem, she added, *For <u>General</u> circulation.*

However, Mrs. Swain continued to harbor anger and resentment toward the Yankees, particularly over what she felt was the worst consequence of the war—the removal of her husband as president of the university.

Lingering anger toward the North was not unusual, explains historian Karen Aviva Rubin: "Most Confederate women 'joined the army,' at least emotionally . . . women were certain at the end of the war that they had been right in their cause. [Many believed] the loss of the war need not necessarily require a readjustment of their feelings about the southern cause, lost or not."

Though Atkins succeeded in winning her over in many ways, Mrs. Swain never gave up one form of protest. She refused to dine with her son-in-law. She would not sit at the dining room table with him when he was a young Union general in the Swain home in April 1865, and she would not eat with him during his many visits to North Carolina and hers to Illinois.

"Three times a day he would carry her meal to her on a tray and sit in her room with her while she ate it," said her great-great-granddaughter "Wuff" Newell. "Then he would go downstairs and eat his meal at the dining table with his wife and children."

Despite her protest, Mrs. Swain and her Yankee son-in-law were bound by their love for Ella.

* * * * *

THE CONTROVERSY over the Swain papers dragged on. Protective and determined as ever, Mrs. Swain moved them from the bank vault to her home in early 1880. Mrs. Spencer continued to plead, ". . . don't give away, & don't burn up those letters & papers we are talking of. You don't know how I long to get my hands on them."

Late the next year, however, Mrs. Swain began to reconsider her position when she learned of a plan to collect and publish North Carolina's colonial records. This had been David Swain's dream.

Finally, Eleanor Swain revised her will:

> The historical collection made by my husband, D.L. Swain, in consideration of his great zeal in providing a good and reliable history of his native State, though unfinished, I leave with the executors of this will to dispose of by a sale, or a gift, as they believe best to ensure a fulfillment of the work to the State of North Carolina.

The new will was dated January 8, 1883.

Then a few days later, she donated the entire collection to the state library.

Her "generous and timely" gift was deemed "for the public benefit," said Secretary of State William L. Saunders. The library's trustees "cannot refrain from expressing their sense of the obligation of the people . . . to Mrs. Swain."

A month later, on February 5, 1883, Eleanor White Swain died.

* * * * *

LISTED AMONG THE ASSETS in Eleanor Swain's estate were farms in Pitt and Edgecombe counties, and in Dalton, Georgia, and a thousand acres of land in Buncombe County, all left to her grandchildren (Ella's three children and Bunkey's daughter, Lula). Her "household goods"—portraits, photographs, and jewelry—were divided among her granddaughters. Dyke inherited her books.

The will stipulated that a "waiting servant, kind and of good morals" be provided "for the care of my youngest and dearest little Susan. . . . The same thing may be done for and by Dot and Dyke, if they like."

Her servants also were remembered: "Matilda, Theny, Sarah, Hetty, Mary, Ermeline, Aunt Dicy Lane, and Dicy & Eliza are the servants I consider in my will to have something." Theny received a teapot, sugar bowl, and a new black Bunting dress. Ollie was left two flannel skirts and was to have "a good black dress bought & given" to her. Sarah received a table with two leaves and three white cane chairs, as well as a coffee grinder and block, and sausage grinder stuffer and bench; Matilda was left a purple woolen shawl; and Mary received a black cashmere dress.

Mrs. Swain requested that a tombstone be placed at Bunkey's grave in Freeport, bearing the inscription, *Sacred to the memory of Richard Caswell Swain, son of Hon. David L. Swain and Eleanor, his wife, of NC. Born Raleigh, 11/28/1837. Died by accident on railroad near Shannon, Ill., Jan. 29, 1872. Erected by his affectionate EHWS of Raleigh, NC.*

She did not forget the debt she believed North Carolina owed her husband: "Money due to me as the sole legatee of my deceased husband,

D.L. Swain, from the trustees of the University of North Carolina, I will to my grandson, S. Dykins Atkins."

Dyke never received the disputed payment. When Mrs. Swain's will was litigated in February 1884, the executors claimed "all debts except one, not admitted to be due, have been paid."

CHAPTER 13

The General

MRS. SWAIN'S DEATH left General Atkins, now forty-seven, with sole responsibility for raising his three children. He also had duties as postmaster, attorney, and community leader. Placing additional demands on his time were his responsibilities at the *Freeport Journal,* which he had repurchased and renamed the *Journal and Republican.*

The Atkinses, no longer traveling south each fall, settled into full-time life in Illinois.

The general remained as deeply committed to his family as ever. In a speech to the New York State Press Association in June 1885, he implored those gathered to "love your wife, and educate your children."

Little did he know that four months later his family would be dealt another blow. On October 27, 1885, his son and namesake, Dyke, died one month shy of his thirteenth birthday.

The general was devastated. "I supposed that I had experienced every phase of suffering inflicted by death upon survivors," he wrote Mrs. Spencer, with whom he occasionally corresponded, "but I have suffered more in the death of my heroic little boy than in all former experiences combined."

The *Journal*'s obituary described young Dyke as

> a lad of unusual promise. The disease of which he died,
> splenetic fever, has kept him in a precarious state of health
> since early in March, when he was attacked with a malignant
> fever, which left him very much reduced in strength; and he
> has since then been subject to sudden and violent relapses,
> increasing in severity with each recurrence.

Despite the severity of his illness, the *Journal* noted, Dyke was able to recognize his loved ones and "the least attention was received with murmured thanks; and when he addressed any one, he never failed to add to their names some title of respect. When the end came . . . a sweet smile rested for an instant upon his features."

Now all of Ella's boys were with her in heaven.

* * * * *

HAVING LOST HIS WIFE and his four sons, General Atkins nevertheless had two daughters to raise. At the time of Dyke's death, Dot was sixteen, and Susie, seven. Both left Freeport to attend school—Dot to Illinois Woman's School in Jacksonville, Illinois, and Susie to Kemper Hall in Kenosha, Wisconsin.

With the girls away, Atkins spent his days running the *Journal*, attending to his civic duties, including service as postmaster, and speaking about his war experiences at various events.

As the years passed, his accomplishments were extensive and noteworthy. He was president of the Stephenson County Old Settlers Association, a member of the Societies of the Army of the Tennessee

General Smith D. Atkins.

and the Army of the Cumberland, and a Mason. To honor him, Freeport's Sons of Veterans No. 400 was named the S.D. Atkins Chapter.

General Atkins's desire to give back to his community was evident
even in his younger days. At nineteen, he had written in his journal:

> Yesterday and today is passed and gone and what have
> I accomplished? Forty-eight hours have been wheeled away
> into eternity . . . and what have I to show for it? Have I done
> anything which will add to the comfort and enjoyment of my
> fellows? . . . What do I accomplish in the live long day that is
> worthy of note? . . . That is a vexed question and one that has
> occupied the minds of men for centuries.

* * * * *

FOR THE REMAINING YEARS OF HIS LIFE, Atkins remained
a widower. "General Atkins never remarried," wrote his great-granddaughter "Wuff" Newell in 1949. "His position as a political leader
required him to attend numerous banquets and social gatherings, but
he was never accompanied by anyone but his oldest daughter."

A few historians believe he did remarry, citing the listing of *Gen.
and Mrs. Smith D. Atkins* as co-hosts of the Fiftieth Anniversary of the
Lincoln-Douglas Debate in 1908. But Edward Finch, Lincoln-Douglas
Society president in 2007, found no mention of a second marriage in
the organization's record: "The entry in the program was an error, probably made by someone who knew Mr. and Mrs. Atkins, and entered
both out of habit."

No records confirm a remarriage. No tombstone in the Freeport
City Cemetery bears the name of Mrs. Smith D. Atkins. No census
records after Ella's death in 1881 list a second wife.

Perhaps General Atkins, himself, provided the answer in *Ninety-Second Illinois Volunteers* when he wrote of falling in love with Miss Ella Swain:

> He went all through the war without being a prisoner, and was captured at last, after the war was over . . . and has been her happy and contented prisoner ever since.

* * * * *

IN 1891, DOT BECAME ENGAGED to Needham Tyndale (Tyn) Cobb of Raleigh. She was twenty-two, the same age her mother had been when she married. The symmetry of the match was striking: A generation after Ella and Genl had married, their daughter—by definition a Northerner, albeit one with strong North Carolina ties—was betrothed to a Southerner.

At the noon wedding December 29, Dot wore her mother's white grosgrain silk wedding dress and carried a bouquet of primrose. Her father was her escort.

Entitled "In Bonds of Love," the *Journal*'s wedding announcement drew parallels between Dot's marriage and that of her parents a generation earlier. Just as the Swain/Atkins wedding was seen as a joining of North and South (at least by those in Freeport), the Atkins/Cobb nuptials united "the hearts and hands of one of the most talented society ladies of this city and one who came far away from the sunny south to claim her for a partner through life."

She had known Tyn, a distant cousin by marriage, since she was a teen staying at her grandmother's home. He was an 1886 graduate of the University of North Carolina—the university once led by the grandfather Dot had never known. Dot and Tyn settled in Raleigh. Early in their marriage, they had a daughter, who died at fourteen months, and two sons—Smith Dykins and Needham Tyndale, Jr.

In 1896, Susie Atkins wed John Loos. The marriage was thought by many to be ill-advised because Loos was considered a ne'er-do-well. The couple had three children and lived for a while on the Pitt County farm Susie had inherited from her grandmother, Eleanor Swain.

Eventually she left Loos and returned to Freeport with her children. General Atkins welcomed them to live with him in his Prospect Terrace home under one condition: The children would take the Atkins name. Susie agreed.

They stayed there until about 1905, when Susie married John Rackley, a Georgia native. They had two children; but that marriage did not last either. In 1910, she and her five children moved home to Freeport, this time for good.

Dot's marriage appears to have been strong, yet plagued with loss. Like her mother and grandmother, Dot suffered the heartbreak of losing children. The Cobbs' last child, named Eleanor Hope, brought renewed happiness when she was born in 1902, six months after the death of a sister, Caroline Irene, not even a year old.

The little girl was called "Hope." Her older brothers were well aware of the family's losses. One morning, Dot found six-year-old Tyn in the children's nursery, standing guard over his new sister, a sheet covering her from head to toe. Dot asked what he was doing. "Making certain the angels don't take this one," he replied.

General Atkins flanked on the left by Dot and her oldest child, Smith, and on the right by Susie and her oldest child, Susie. Dot is wearing her mother's cameo, inscribed *Ella from Smith Oct. 25ᵗʰ, 1871.*

* * * * *

WHEN GENERAL ATKINS neared retirement in 1906, Dot, Tyn, and their three children also moved to Freeport to the Prospect Terrace home. Though he never entirely handed over the reins of the *Journal,* Atkins made son-in-law Tyn managing editor. The paper now enjoyed a reputation for "aggressiveness and at the same time a fairness that is commendable," wrote *National Printer–Journalist* editor, B.B. Herbert.

Under the general's guidance, the *Journal* had grown from six columns to standard size, "with seven columns to the page, and from eight to sixteen pages per issue," Herbert noted. For many years it was the town's only newspaper "which espoused the cause of the people . . . a newspaper so fearless in the interest of the common good. . . ."

It wasn't just loyalty to Freeport that made General Atkins a good newspaperman. He was dedicated to accuracy, as was evident in the way he trained those who would follow him. Herbert observed:

> He disliked sensational methods . . . and when the younger members of the staff, on such important occasions as a disastrous cloud-burst in the county, or the sinking of the Titanic, ventured to "break the columns" and spread the news over more than one column in width, they never breathed easy until they knew whether the General disapproved of a departure from the old conservative ideals.

The general remained a popular speaker. People loved hearing his honest and vivid stories about his war experiences. On February 22, 1907, he addressed the Women's Relief Corps in Mendota, Illinois, about the Battle of Chickamauga. The subtitle of his speech was "Useless, Disastrous Battle":

> On August 16th, 1863, when the movement of the Army of the Cumberland began . . . against the Army of the Confederacy under Bragg at Chattanooga, I was not . . . informed of the plans of the campaign for I held only the rank of colonel of a single regiment, and a boy at that. . . . The object of the campaign was the capture of Chattanooga. I am not an educated soldier; I am not capable of making any technical criticism of military campaigns. . . .
>
> The useless battle had been fought, the useless sacrifice of thousands of brave men of the Army of the Cumberland had been made. . . . The volunteer soldiers were not only brave, but they were sensible always. They complained very loudly when they had a right to complaint [sic], and they submitted to every hardship without complaint when there was necessity for it. . . .

Later that year, he spoke at the Abraham Lincoln Centre in Chicago at the dedication of the John A. Davis Room, honoring a soldier with whom Smith Atkins had fought at Shiloh. The general remembered his fallen comrade, assuring Davis's family he "bore well his part," even dictating to Atkins his account of the battle while in terrible pain from his wounds.

Because General Atkins was vice president of the Illinois State Historical Society, he was asked to speak at the fiftieth anniversary celebration of the Lincoln-Douglas debate held in Freeport. As a young newspaperman covering the event, Atkins had been in the same room with Lincoln after he arrived in town:

> . . . his room, at the Brewster House . . . was soon crowded. . . . There was no formal conference, no formal consultation of Republicans. . . . The door of Mr. Lincoln's room stood wide open, and anyone came or went as he pleased. When I entered the room Mr. Lincoln was washing his face, and putting on a clean shirt and the conversation was general.

At the February 12, 1909, "Tribute of a Century to Lincoln," General Atkins— introduced as "a contemporary and personal acquaintance" of the sixteenth president—told the crowd, "I knew Abraham Lincoln before he went to Washington as President, he studied every question thoroughly, & was absolutely honest."

Atkins's speeches always conveyed his devotion to home and country. In Herbert's 1912 comments on the *Journal*, he talked of the general's love for Freeport, underscored in the closing line of his editorials: *Good ole Freeport, City of homes, churches and schools.* Herbert also emphasized his "influence on the newspapers of the Midwest . . . there is none more widely quoted nor more highly respected."

* * * *

B Y 1913, GENERAL ATKINS had been editor and principal owner of the *Journal* and served as postmaster for nearly fifty years. On March 27 of that year, his long, full life ended at the Prospect Terrace home he once had shared with Ella.

He had been ill for ten days and nursed by Dot. Finally, on the evening of the 27th, he "fell asleep," the *Journal* reported. "There was no struggle; he was willing to and ready to go and so expressed himself just before he lapsed into unconsciousness."

General Atkins's obituary emphasized his leadership abilities as a soldier, businessman, and suitor of the young Southern woman who would become his wife:

> He was an ardent Republican, a student of political economy, and having his long life time seen so much of history in the making, his experience enabled him to see the shaping of things ahead; and, more than once, while seemingly his entire clientele differed with him, later it was admitted that he was in the right.

His long-time minister, the Reverend F.J. Bates, of Grace Episcopal Church, gave the eulogy:

> Those who knew him knew also that he thought carefully and long before he spoke, and having once spoken, would never withdraw, save on the new conviction that he had been wrong.

He was consulted often on large questions, and his memory of events of even more than half a century ago was little short of wonderful. His mind was a book of facts that were part of a virile history of his times. His times—particularly the era of wartime—called for all the strength that men possessed, and his contribution was memorable and worthy.

Atkins's contributions to his hometown were well known, but "his title of 'Grandfather' will mean more than that of 'General,'" Bates noted. "His heart was as the heart of a child in many things, and therefore he loved little children, his own with intensest enjoyment, and was loved by them in adequate return."

These observations echo those of Ella, who had once written her parents of her husband lovingly rocking and singing little David to sleep, bouncing him on the bed, drumming on the bottom of a pail to the child's delight, "playing and romping. . . . [He is] so good to <u>both</u> your <u>babies Ella</u> & David just as good as he can be."

Publisher, historian, and friend Richard V. Carpenter described the general's nature as "a positive one; when he thought a thing should be done so and so, it was usually done, but his influence was for the good, his judgment correct, and his work was directed to building up his country and . . . Freeport. . . ."

* * * * *

ENERAL ATKINS wanted a simple funeral, open to all soldiers, especially members of the Ninety-second Illinois. Simple it might have been. But its size was "the largest ever held in Freeport," reported the *Journal.* "The large rooms of the home were filled and many stood on the lawn as the citizens passed through to view their old friend for the last time."

That Sunday afternoon, visitors entering the library of the Atkins home to pay their respects walked across a rug fashioned from the Brussels carpet upon which he and Ella had stood during their wedding nearly fifty years earlier.

His casket was surrounded by flowers and telegrams, including one from the Typographical Union, to which *Journal* typesetters belonged. The telegram ended with *30*—newspaper symbol for "the end."

Fittingly, mourners were reminded not only of the war heroism of this former Yankee general, but also of his ties to the South, as "several stirring war songs" were played on the very piano "which had been played at the marriage of General Atkins to the Governor's daughter."

Among the general's pallbearers were the town's six oldest letter carriers in uniform. They marched from the Atkins home to the Freeport City Cemetery and were followed by the carrier boys for the *Journal.* The paper reported, "The little fellows, of their own accord, met at the Journal office and marched to the house, viewed the remains . . . and marched in the procession." Other postal employees and newspaper staff joined the procession to the cemetery where General Atkins was buried "under a mound several times covered with the most beautiful flowers . . . by the side of his father and mother."

Buried with him was the headquarters flag of the Second Brigade of Kilpatrick's Cavalry, "the one used in the march from Atlanta to the sea, and through the Carolina's to the end of the war." A Union flag draped the casket, and "Taps" was played.

His headstone was made from a piece of granite on which type had once been set for the *Journal*'s pages. On it was carved the following:

> Smith Dykins Atkins. Born June 9, 1835. Married Aug. 23, 1865 To Eleanor Hope Swain. Died March 27, 1913. First soldier to enlist for the Civil War, in Stephenson County. Colonel 92nd Ill. Vols. His children and his children's children rise up and call him blessed. This stone was used by him in his newspaper work when a printer. He was for nearly half century editor of the *Freeport Journal*.

That he was buried in Freeport and his beloved Ella in Raleigh was of little consequence. As Ella once had written to her mother after Baby Graham and Little David had died:

> I . . . take life as it is measured out to me, with no look into the future except at the close, when my boys shall come again, when God shall send them to bring their mother home, and that home will never be desolate.

Nearly half a century after courageously promising to love one another until death did them part, Ella and her Genl were finally home.

Notes

CHAPTER ONE —A Wooing Begins

1   *Easter Sunday 1865 in Chapel Hill*
    Spencer, *The Last*, 150, 170.

1   *The small Southern town*
    Battle, *History*, Vol. 1, 1; Mallett, Excerpts.

1   *Intensifying fears were reports*
    Lyman, 76–79; Committee, 211. Kilpatrick reportedly told officers in his com-
    mand during a January 27, 1865, party near Savannah, Georgia, "In after years,
    when travellers passing through South Carolina shall see the chimney stacks
    without houses, and the country desolate, and shall ask, Who did this?
    some Yankee will answer, Kilpatrick's cavalry."

1   *Everyone had thought Chapel Hill*
    Battle, *Memories*, 199; Guernsey and Alden, 713.

2   *Chapel Hillians prepared for*
    Battle, *Memories*, 198; Vickers, 72; Battle, *History*, Vol. 1, 336, 409.

2   *"Between sundown and dark…"*
    Mallett, Excerpts; Spencer, *The Last*, 171; Wills, 371–72.

3   *Though some estimated the*
    Dollar; Chamberlain, 84; Spencer, *The Last*, 171; Graham, *Papers*, Vol. 6,
    306–07. Swain reported that General Kilpatrick had provided a permanent
    guard for UNC for twenty days, with mounted men patrolling the streets
    at night and citizens having soldiers quartered in their homes, upon request.

3   *The soldiers were a tired bunch*
    Murray, 509; Russell, 56; Dollar; Spencer, *The Last*, 173; Committee, 240.

They camped near Morrisville Station, now Morrisville, which had seen little bloodshed during the war.

3   *Meanwhile, Wheeler's troops*
Graham, *Papers*, Vol. 6, 286; Chamberlain, 84. Swain wrote Graham on March 23, 1865, "Some 600 Cavalry passed here on Sunday belonging to Hampton's division and squads of Wheeler's men have been going through at intervals ever since. They demean themselves quietly, notwithstanding one of our citizens sends out to them small quantities of whiskey. Some 50 mounted men and a long wagon train are passing while I write."

3   *Among the young women*
Swain Bible; Battle, *History*, Vol. 1, 425–26, 467; Swain, E.W., Unpublished, February 4, 1862; Powell, *The First*, 65; "The Fire," *University Magazine;* Spencer, *North Carolina Presbyterian.* The house was built in 1810 by Helen Hogg Hooper Caldwell. It served as the President's House when her second husband, Joseph Caldwell, was university president. After the Caldwells died, the house had several occupants before becoming the Swains' home in 1848. It was destroyed in a fire on Christmas day 1886 and rebuilt in 1907. Today it is the home of the president of the University of North Carolina system.

4   *At the start of the war*
Madden, 33. Ray survived the war, became a lieutenant, and later was elected to the Georgia State Legislature.

4   *Students were not the only ones*
Swain, E.W., Unpublished, February 4, 1862; Battle, *History*, Vol. 1, 723.

4   *Ella's own brother*
Barile; Battle, *History*, Vol. 1, 575; Swain, E.W., Unpublished, February 4, 1862. Battle notes that young Richard was "known as 'Little Bunk'" after his father's nickname, "Old Bunk," given him as a young man because he was from Buncombe County, North Carolina.

5   *Bunkey was one of the lucky*
Russell, 48; Battle, *History*, Vol. 1, 745; Swain, E.W., Unpublished, February 4, 1862.

6   *Not only had Chapel Hillians*
Swain, E.W., Unpublished, February 4, 1862; Battle, *History*, Vol. 1, 745, 750–51.

6   *Residents, like many others*
Jones, J.B., *A Rebel*, 386; Spencer, *The Last*, 30; Graham, *Papers*, Vol. 6, 286. Union soldiers were not the only ones to deplete Chapel Hill's stores. Swain wrote Graham March 23, 1865, "Some of my neighbors have been constrained

to furnish inconvenient supplies of corn, as well as long forage, and we will all breathe more freely when it shall be ascertained that all are through."

6   *The women who remained*
Russell, 46.

6   *In spite of the war's*
Battle, *History,* Vol. 1, 737; Brewer, *Memoir of*; Perry, *Reminiscences,* 192.

7   *When Wheeler's men streamed*
Russell, 56, 60; Spencer, *The Last,* 166, 171.

7   *Surrender was bitter, but*
Barile, letter from Susan White to Anna and Ella, August 1863.

8   *No one understood the*
Graham, *Papers,* Vol. 6, 285–304; Swain, "Address"; Spencer, *The Last,* 147–51. It took much convincing to get Governor Vance to agree to surrender, especially after a bill to arm slaves became law in March 1865. Vance called for a General Assembly meeting to discuss it. Graham wrote Swain on March 26 that he believed Vance was "unequal" to the crisis. Swain responded on April 8 that perhaps he and Graham should meet with him. Graham replied, "I left Richmond thoroughly satisfied, that . . . Independence for the Southern Confederacy was perfectly hopeless . . . [and it] was the duty of State Government immediately to move for the purpose of effecting an adjustment of the quarrel with the United States."

The next day Vance suggested the General Assembly elect commissioners to broker a treaty, and that if Sherman entered Raleigh that he [Vance] would send a commission to treat with him for a suspension of hostilities until the State could take further action to end the war. Vance sent a telegram to Graham on April 11 asking to meet with him. Graham arrived in Raleigh at 3 AM to meet with the Governor and Swain. Then Swain and Graham wrote General Sherman to request an interview.

On April 12, Vance again wrote Sherman to tell him Raleigh Mayor William B. Harrison was authorized to surrender the capital and asked safe passage for commission members, Graham and Swain. Sherman issued such an order. Commissioners boarded a train at 10:30 AM on April 12, but it was stopped by Confederate forces and ordered back to Raleigh. Then Union soldiers stopped it and escorted the two former governors to Sherman's headquarters "in the field" near Raleigh. Because of delays, they did not return to Raleigh until the next day, April 13. Vance had already abandoned the city.

On May 6, Swain wrote Graham that he was sorry Vance had not returned to Raleigh: "I am satisfied that so far as Gen'l Sherman is concerned he would have been permitted to continue in the discharge of executive duties, until the Legislature could have convened, called a Convention, and organized the government, under the new regime." Graham concurred, noting that Vance's request to send a commission to Washington, DC, had been rejected. "The Governor was told he need not apprehend any arrest by the military, and might go where he pleased."

9 *Back home two days later*
Chamberlain, 84–85; Spencer, *The Last*, 165–70.

10 *How would the town that*
Spencer, *The Last*, 170–71; Committee, 242; Battle, *History*, Vol. 1, 743.

10 *By birth, wrote Kemp Battle*
Battle, "Wilson," 315–18; Walbert. Walbert notes, "Wilson Swain Caldwell [was] . . . born into slavery . . . his mother was Rosa Burgess, a slave of the University of North Carolina President David Swain. . . . Under the laws of the day, children born to slaves were the property of their mother's master. Wilson Caldwell was originally owned by President Swain, thus his name was Wilson Swain until Emancipation, at which point he took his father's last name. . . . [He] grew up alongside the son of David Swain, Richard Caswell Swain (1837–1872), whereby Caldwell received some education—a rare opportunity for slaves at that time. Caldwell was not treated as a slave but as a playmate and part of the family." Wilson Swain Caldwell later served on the Chapel Hill town council.

10 *Captain Schermerhorn announced that*
Committee, 242; Battle, "Wilson," 315–18; Spencer, *The Last*, 170–71; Perry, *The War*, 215.

10 *It was a peaceful surrender*
Committee, 242; Russell, 56; Spencer, *The Last*, 171.

10 *Brigade commander for the feared*
Russell, 62; Lyman, 76–79; Atkins, "With Sherman's," 386; Smith, 82.

11 *Raised on a farm outside*
Carpenter, 82; Atkins, Personal Journal, November 22, 1854; "David Lowry Swain." Atkins was the namesake of his mother's father, Smith Dykins.

11 *Smith Atkins started practicing law*
Carpenter, 82; *In the Footprints*, 21.

11 *He had grown up hearing*
In the Footprints, 22; Fernow; Atkins Bible (Smith D.).

11 *At age twenty-five, he*
"April 1861—Proclamations"; Fulwider, 239; *In the Footprints*, 22, 29.

12 *Out of deference to his host*
Atkins, "Democracy"; Fulwider, 239. Fulwider notes, "The firing on Fort
Sumter, while not a surprise, presented a new situation. The issue was no
longer slavery, it was the preservation of the National Union. While Stephenson County had been sharply divided on the various issues arising out of the
slavery question, her people stood almost a unit on the greater question of the
preservation of the Union, and how well they did their part in the greatest
crisis of the nation is written in the history of her fighting men on the battlefield. Party lines were practically obliterated and Democrats and Republicans
went to the front side by side, not to free the negroes, but to save a nation."

12 *On the April morning President*
Graham, *Papers*, Vol. 6, 309; United States, Census; Swain Bible.

12 *The Swains referred to their slaves*
Swain Bible; Chapel of the Cross Record Book.

13 *Offering to show his guest*
Russell, 62–63; Carpenter, 84.

13 *His daughter Ella, a faithful*
Russell, 63, 284–86; Carpenter, 84; Holmes; Tepper, 134–35; Smith, 82. In
1942, playwright Holmes imagined in "At the Crossroads on the Hill" Atkins
declaring his love: "I will soon return to Freeport," [Atkins said] as he and
Ella strolled arm-in-arm down the sidewalk past Chapel of the Cross. "But
I shall mark well the road between there and Chapel Hill, long and difficult
as it is . . . Eleanor! For I hope you will let me call you so, without all this
formality. Have I been slow in caring for you here in this awkward situation
that confronts us? Have I not appointed a special guard to see to it that the
functions of this University shall go undisturbed. . . . I would like to hope that
you would let me surround you with ever greater protection—when you come
to Freeport. . . .
"I know that I should not say what I now wish to say without first speaking
to your father, but he will understand. I want you to come to Freeport—as—
Mrs. Atkins—my wife. . . . Eleanor dear, if your father does not oppose it,
will you go with me to Illinois?"
Ella's reply, Holmes suggested, was as Atkins had hoped, though guarded:
"I think I will dear—Smith. But we must say no more about this until we have
spoken to father."
UNC professor Bland Simpson and Jack Herrick of the Red Clay Ramblers,
a Chapel Hill music group, produced "Tar Heel Voices: A Musical 200th" for
UNC's Bicentennial Celebration. "The Ballad of Ellie Swain" tells of Ella and
the general's love affair.
Tepper recounts, "Standing alone in the foreground, wearing a long, beauti-
ful dress of lavender chiffon, Ellie Swain gave voice to the melancholy ballad.

Behind her, words of one song—staged as a ballet—were acted out in
a dreamy haze: 'And their horses are stabled on our campus, And their picket-
lines are stationed on our hill, And their uniforms are bluer than our heaven.
They say they'll never leave. . . . And I think they never will.'"

C H A P T E R   T W O — Poetry & Prejudice

19 *Kilpatrick's brigade made itself*
Committee, 246–47; Peters, "History." Singing was a popular pastime. In his
"Beloit Address," delivered at the Sons of Veterans campfire, Atkins reminisced,
"One day I was riding through the camps of the Union soldiers where there
were literally thousands . . . engaged in all sorts of employment—some were
writing letters home, some were mending their clothing, some were pitching
quoits, some were playing baseball, some were reading old newspapers, and
a glee club was singing and thousands of voices joined in the chorus. What
do you think those Union soldiers were singing in their far-away camps, by
the slowly flowing southern rivers, in the shadow of the southern mountains?
Listen, I will tell you: 'Christ among the lilies, / Was born across the sea, /
With a glory in his bosom, / That transgresses you and me, / As He died to
make men holy, / Let us die to make men free, / Glory, glory, hallelujah! /
As we go marching on.'"

20 *Those words were the most "unpopular*
Committee, 246–47.

20 *The general hardly noticed*
Atkins, Personal Journal; Barile. The acrostic was not Atkins's first attempt to
write poetry, as he noted in his journal: this "specimen of my shallow 'poetry'
on shallow fame—shallow world—shallow, shallow, shallow. And will all
this shallow evening's shallow writing be the shallow memento to leave
behind to remember me of the 9th and 10th of November 1854. Well may it
do my shallow self good if in years to come I will even be so shallow as to
reperuse [*sic*] it: Fame only dwells on Fortune's giddy wheel; / At every turn
it's lost and won again. / Why then wrestle in the false ordeal, / Or deem the
shadowy phantom real. / Always true worth is courted but in vain. / Many
noble hearts have strove life-long, / Died, and were forgotten, as the giddy
throng. / Still, even the fame of Fortune, any fame, / Throws a certain halo
'round ones name. / Fortune, Fame! Oh, were I your slave / To ride forever the
eternal sea / And sport familiar with thy crested wave / And only dream of
emmortality [*sic*]—/ Bright hope! Dame Fortune be not blind, / Blast not this
dear creation of my mind?"

Atkins's desire for love is clear in his February 14, 1855, journal entry: "St. Valentine's Day. But Cupid is a partial rogue and I have not been favored with a single line by him. But the muses never favored me in any audible way and save the side glances of now and then an ideal Minerva, no other. . . . Kind Cupid deal gently with me; withhold the bounty now but forget me not and by and by copiously shower on me and mine thy most joyous smiles!"

21 *After presenting it to her*
Isaac. Years later he wrote Cockley that "in the well thumbed copy of it still preserved by the matronly 'Mrs. S.D. Atkins' the second line of the last verse appears with the above changes."

22 *With great pleasure, Ella*
Spencer, "Letter from," May 12, 1865.

22 *She coyly returned Atkins's*
Atkins, E.H.S., Autograph Book. Atkins's infatuation was evident years later when he wrote in the front of her Autograph Book: *Mrs. Smith D. Atkins née Eleanor H. Swain.*

23 *Not everyone in Chapel Hill*
Mallett, Excerpt; Newell, "Ellie Swain's"; Swain, E.W., Unpublished to Selina Wheat, February 4, 1862, and from Mary Gatlin, November 18, 1865; Culpepper, 2; United States, Census; Spencer Papers, Mrs. Spencer to Mrs. Swain, March 13, 1872. Mrs. Wheat was wife of John T. Wheat, former professor and Chapel of the Cross rector, who had moved to Arkansas.

25 *The village of Chapel Hill had paid*
Spencer, *The Last*, 263; Battle, *History*, Vol. 1, 733.

26 *President Swain had struggled*
"A Nursery of Patriotism"; Barile, letter from Emma C. White to Anne and Ella, August 20, 1863.

27 *Conditions at the university*
Spencer, *The Last*, 179; Committee, 243.

27 *So extreme was the deprivation*
Spencer, *The Last*, 179; Committee, 243.

27 *As her father tried to improve*
Spencer, "Letter from," May 12, 1865.

28 *Two weeks after Ella Swain*
Committee, 247–49.

29 *During the weeks of waiting*
Chamberlain, 98; Committee, 248–51.

CHAPTER THREE — The Talk & the Curse of the Town

33 *Word of Ella Swain's betrothal*
Russell, 67; Battle, *History*, Vol. 1, 744; Barile; Vickers, 73; Britton, 321; Silber, 129–30; Spencer, "Letter from," May 12, 186; Graham, *Papers*, Vol. 6, 306. Swain's interactions with Atkins had been pleasant. He wrote Graham on May 6, 1865, that he saw a bay mare taken from his stable. He complained to Atkins, who "assured me that the command should not move before he ferreted her out, and contrary to my expectations he found her and delivered her some days afterwards. . . . My premises were not trespassed upon in any other instance, and we have experienced not merely protection, but remarkable quiet. I have known the time when my boys could create more disturbance, noise and confusion in an hour, than Gen'l Atkins brigade have exhibited in a week." Britton and Silber both address the frequency of North-South marriages— Yankee boys to Southern girls—following the war.

34 *A generation earlier, the Swains'*
Waugh, 37; Murray, 206, 216; Cobb Loan, December 29, 1824; Brewer, 4, 7. (See also family tree.) Mrs. Swain did not know her famous maternal grandfather and his wife who died before her birth. Her paternal grandparents died when she was three. She may have been unaware that David Swain's uncle, Joel Lane, was the founder of Raleigh, and that his cousin Joseph Lane was a U.S. senator and governor of Oregon.

34 *David Swain came from a well-respected*
Barile; Bye, 95–98; "David Lowry Swain"; Cobb Loan, George Swain to Judge Taylor, April 29, 1823. (See also family tree.) Arthur E. Bye, professional restorer hired in 1943 by the university to restore the oil portraits, wrote in his appraisal of Swain's: "Notice how painstakingly and honest the hands are executed. . . . One of the visitors to my studio, upon seeing this picture for the first time, exclaimed: 'How like Lincoln it is!' And President Swain was like Lincoln; he arose from the same background, and remained the plain, rugged, honest, thoughtful, and deep-seeing man."

36 *These traits could be attributed*
Spencer Papers; Spencer, "Proceedings," 52, and Mrs. Spencer to Mrs. Swain, January 17, 1869; Cobb Loan, W.R. Gales to Swain, August 9, 1823, and March 24, 1824, Dr. R.B. Vance to Swain, November 18, 1823, and Swain to Eleanor White, December 29, 1824; Battle, *History*, Vol. 1, 534. After Swain's death, Mrs. Spencer was asked to write a sketch of his life for the Proceedings of the Grand Masonic Lodge of North Carolina. Mrs. Swain was a major source for her piece. Mrs. Spencer wrote, "He retained through life the pure and simple habits and tastes, and the moderation which were inculcated at home. His father was ambitious for him, and ambitious of the best things. He taught his son to choose good company and to aim high."

37   *Buoyed by their encouragement*
     Cobb Loan, December 29, 1824.

38   *Ten days later, on January 12*
     Swain Bible; Barile; Cobb Loan; Spencer, "Proceedings." White Hall, now
     called White-Holman House, still stands in Raleigh. It was moved in the
     mid-1980s to New Bern Place, a block from its original location. It has been
     converted to office space.

40   *The newlyweds promptly moved*
     Spencer, "Proceedings"; Cobb Loan.

41   *He longed to be with her*
     Barile; Cobb Loan, David Swain to Eleanor Swain, August 11, 1826, August 25,
     1826, September 8, 1826, September 22, 1826, October 2, 1826, October 27, 1826,
     March 18 and 22, 1827, January 1, 1828, January 20, 1828, March 21, 1828, and
     August 7, 1828; Perry, *Reminiscences*, 191; Swain Bible; "David Lowry Swain."
     Former South Carolina Governor Benjamin F. Perry notes, "Whilst reading
     law at the capital of the State, Governor Swain became engaged to a young
     lady of that city, whom he afterwards married. This induced him to give up
     his native mountain home."
        There are no extant letters from Mrs. Swain to her husband. She may not
     have been as faithful a correspondent as he. He urged her in a March 18, 1827,
     letter to write him every week, and noted four days later, "I feel great anxiety
     about your health."
        The Swains had a loving marriage. In 1857 when Swain was experiencing
     hearing loss, Eleanor wrote daughter Anne following his successful treatment:
     "Pa exclaimed what makes you talk so loud. This overstraining of the voice,
     which had almost become a custom, was almost as much relief to me as Pa
     hearing to him—surely we have much to be thankful for."

41   *In Ella's match with General Atkins*
     Wells; Culpepper, 391; Cobb Loan, letters from David Swain to Eleanor
     Swain; Leonard, 173. (See also family tree.) Culpepper notes, "With the return
     of peace, some women welcomed their husbands home and promptly settled
     back into their former 'cult of domesticity.' Other women, however, had been
     awakened by their war experiences to a host of their own unexplored talents
     and to a much wider world beyond their immediate family and neighbors."

41   *Mrs. Swain saw great promise*
     Swain, E.W., Unpublished, February 19, 1857; Caldwell, 196; Edmunds;
     Barile, Richard Sterling to Ella, November 14, 1860; Graham, *Papers*, Vol. 5,
     111; Spencer Papers, letter to Eleanor Swain, August 26, 1881. Swain wrote
     Graham on August 8, 1859, that he would probably bring Ella to the Graham
     house that week on her way to school in Greensboro.

43 *About this time, Ella became*
Swain, E.W., Unpublished, February 4, 1862; New Testament; Chapel of the
Cross Record Book. Mrs. Swain believed strongly in salvation, writing in her
Bible, "The Certainty of the resurrection dispels the gloom of the grace. . . .
A mere sight of Divine power drives us away from God; as insight of His
power and love drives us near to him." From the Chapel of the Cross Record
Book: "Anne Caroline Swain, David Lowry Swain and Richard Caswell
Swain, children of David and Eleanor, were baptized October 12th, 1840, by
Rev. W.M. Green." David died three days later.

43 *After leaving Edgeworth, Ella*
Scott, General Introduction; Stoops, 20; Faust, "Altars," 172; Faust, *Mothers*, xiii; Rable, 19; Sterkx, 17; Battle, *History*, Vol. 1, 347. Records prior to
1885 were destroyed in a fire. St. Mary's founder Rev. Smedes believed that a
young woman's "mission . . . has not been generally felt and understood. . . .
she has therefore been sent forth on her high vocation, too often entirely
ignorant of her responsibilities, and utterly unfit to discharge them." He called
for "a broad and deep foundation . . . in those departments of study which
strengthen and establish the mind, and improve the reasoning faculties."
    Faust, Rable, and Sterkx all note that a limited education was considered
preferable for Southern women.

44 *Ella wrote to Mrs. Spencer*
Spencer, "Letter from," May 12, 1865.

44 *But word of the engagement*
UNC Bicentennial, 10; Jones, H.G., *North Carolina*, 263; Powell, *The First*, 89;
Barrett, 265; Bradley, 245; Russell, 69; Battle, *History*, Vol. 1, 744.

45 *Further provoking public outrage*
Chamberlain, 142; UNC Bicentennial, 10; Battle, *History*, Vol. 1, 779; Daniels,
"University"; Spencer, *The Last*, 55.

45 *Even though Mrs. Spencer had*
Chamberlain, 98; Powell, *The First*, 89.

46 *General Atkins felt he had*
Spencer, *The Last*, 170–71; Perry, *The War*, 248; Committee, 245.

47 *Atkins became a lightning rod*
Spencer, *The Last*, 173; UNC Bicentennial, 10; Mallet, Excerpts; Graham,
Papers, Vol. 6, 310; Bradley, 245; Barrett, 265; Graham, John W., letter to
David Swain; Battle, *Memories*, 199. Bradley notes, Mrs. Jones of Hillsbor-
ough, widow of Col. Cadwallader Jones, accused Brevet Brig. General Thomas
J. Jordan's servants of stealing silver when Jordan stayed in her home. When
Jordan could not find it, he paid her for it. Barrett notes that she accused

Atkins of the theft; her son Dr. Jones later wrote lawyer and politician John Graham, Governor Graham's son, authorizing him to tell Swain that no silver was taken during Atkins's stay. There's no record of Atkins staying in the Jones home; the regiment's official records show only that the men camped near Hillsborough on May 4.

The Jones rumor apparently reached President Swain. *Fayetteville Observer* editor E.J. Hale, who resented Swain's implication that he had spread that rumor, wrote Swain on June 20, 1866: "I do not think it a friendly act towards either of us to connect me, particularly with such a story (in which you have a personal interest). . . . If I had heard the stories I should not have doubted it. . . . how should I doubt it? Did we not have many instances in our own town of grand and petty larcenies by as high officers even our corps commanders—a rank above General Atkins, I believe."

Kemp Plummer Battle (UNC president 1876–91) recalled, "A cavalry brigade under General Atkins did reach Chapel Hill and encamped in the woods adjoining our house. Mother became uneasy and let the silver down our well tied up in a bag. The troops used the well two or three weeks but did not find the bag."

Mrs. Spencer noted, "I suppose you know that there are people in N.C. yet who believe Ellie was married in finery that Gen Atkins had taken from N.C. ladies. I remember Gov Swain showing me a letter that he received to that effect. He would shake his head over such things & let them pass. No need to contradict such things. But there are plenty of people now who would be glad to know the marriage had turned out badly. I don't care for such. . . ."

Swain wrote Graham on June 1, 1866, that Edmund Cooper of Tennessee, serving as acting private secretary to Andrew Johnson, "spoke to me in high terms of him [Atkins] as an officer and a man." Battle noted in *History* that Atkins "ingratiated himself with our people by his fairness and courtesy. He was a man of fine appearance and of high character."

CHAPTER FOUR—A General Is Born

49   *To ease some of the anxiety*
Freeport Journal, "General Atkins"; Graham, *Papers,* Vol. 6, 318; Smith, 82. The *Journal* reported that Swain "visited General Atkins' home in Illinois." Smith notes, "During the summer [Ella's] father visited General Atkins' home in Illinois and satisfied himself as to his character and social standing." Swain was in New York City in late June/early July, per his July 4, 1865, letter to Graham.

51   *The Atkins family arrived*
Battle, *History*, Vol. 1, 744; Atkins Bible (Smith D.); *In the Footprints*, 20–21;
Atkins, Personal Journal; *Portrait and Biographical Album*, 189–90. Adna
Stanly Atkins, born in New Haven, Connecticut, New Year's Day 1790, was
eleven years older than Swain. According to his obituary, as a young man,
he "apprenticed to learn the tailoring trade, and served out his full time at the
business in Philadelphia. Being naturally of a roving disposition, he started
out on an extended tour of observation at the conclusion of his apprenticeship,
and spent several years abroad. . . . At the time of the breaking out of the war
of 1812 he was in England, and at the first alarm he hastened back to his native
country and joined the United States army."

52   *The situation between the North*
Guernsey and Alden, 61; "April 1861—Proclamations"; Carpenter, 83. Atkins's
U.S. Army Commission, signed by Abraham Lincoln, is in possession of
Atkins's great-great-grandsons, sons of Smith Dykins Atkins Cobb Jr.

53   *He was not disappointed*
Guernsey and Alden, 227, 235, 299; Gustason, "A Tale"; *In the Footprints*, 29;
Freeport Journal, April 21, 1894; Hurlbut, 109; Fulwider, 6; Carpenter, 83;
Barile. Atkins enlisted on April 17, 1861, with Company A, Eleventh Illinois
Volunteers. According to *In the Footprints*, "No community exhibited greater
patriotism than Stephenson county during the civil war. Scarcely had the
smoke at Sumter cleared away before active preparations for war began. On
April 18th a meeting was held at Plymouth Hall in which patriotism obscured
party affiliations. All were American for the defence of the country and the
flag. . . . Speeches by S.D. Atkins, Charles Betts, C.S. Bragg and William
Wagner aroused the patriotic enthusiasm to fever heat. . . . Within two days
the first company [roster] was filled [and] ready for muster."
    Atkins wrote friend John L. Bittinger from the Fourth Division of Army
of the Tennessee, Three Rivers, Hastings, Savannah, Tennessee, on March 12,
1862: "We had a very hard time at Fort Henry, lying out in the snow and rain
six nights without tents, and at the siege of Fort Donelson we suffered almost
everything; and I am in fact very much surprised that I went through with
that terrible exposure, saying nothing about the hazzards [*sic*] of the battle.
And, John, that was a terrible fight. I know what it is now to hear bullets whit-
tle around my ears like hail that do not spare one's friends & comrades, but cut
them down like grain before the silo—what it is to help a wounded man away,
to cover up a dead comrade with a blanket, or stumble over his dead body in
the heat of the fighting. . . . I ride a splendid iron grey four year old, one of the
captured horses at Fort Donelson . . . & you would slightly 'smile' to see me
'swell' when 'myself' and Genl Hurlbut with our staff 'ride out'. . . . I wait to
go through the expected fight—somewhere this side of Florence, Ala., which
is said to promise to be a harder one than Donelson, the rebels being in force

with 50,000 troops & unlimited means of reinforcements. Then I think I will quit—'seeking the baubles, reputation, at the canons mouth'—and quietly subside into civil life and obscurity at Freeport, or some meaner town if I can find one."

54 *Atkins's heroic performance*
Freeport Journal, April 21, 1894; Winship, 71; "Overview of the Civil War."

55 *No sooner had the Ninety-second*
Atkins, "With Sherman's"; *Freeport Journal*, April 21, 1894, March 18, 1912; Baumgartner, 59; Atkins, Personal notes; "Engagement Chronology"; *In the Footprints*, 29–30; Finkelman, 78. Atkins's soldiers used the first Spencer Repeating Rifles during the battles. At Bentonville, the Ninety-second massed on the left side around dusk March 19.

58 *Despite his success on the*
Atkins, Personal Journal, February 17, 1855.

58 *But Smith Atkins the Civil War*
"General Atkins Beloit Address." He told the crowd of being invited to give the Fourth of July address at Durand, Illinois: "Just before the meeting a farm wagon was drawn close to the stand, and an old gentleman was lifted out of the wagon onto the stand and it was stated that he had been a soldier in the American Revolutionary War. I remember with what great veneration all the people looked upon that venerable man. I will never forget my own emotions. I was disposed to think it very hard that while Washington and the Continental soldiers in the American Revolution had a chance to fight for their country, my life was in peaceful times, and I should have no opportunity to serve my country on the battlefield. Little did I dream at the time that the great Civil war was so near when all would have a chance to serve their country.

"You will never know—you never can know—what your fathers so well knew and felt when the clouds of war gathered in 1861. How they did come, the volunteers, from every walk in life, the sunbrowned farmer boys from their fields; the clerks from the store; the bookkeeper from his counting house; the pale student from his school or college; the lawyer from his office; even the ministers of the gospel from their pulpits, until the ranks were full, and there was no room for them, and they were turned homeward again. But their patriotism never ended, it only grew stronger. . . . We wonder at the calmness and patience of George Washington, never furnished with the troops that were needed, the soldiers constantly deserting and going home, never properly clothed, or fed, or paid, or furnished with proper arms. . . ."

59 *A postmaster's position would*
Brewer, 3; "Abraham Lincoln Chronology." President Swain's father served as Asheville, North Carolina, postmaster, 1806–29. Lincoln also had been a postmaster in the early 1830s in Salem, Illinois.

CHAPTER 5 — Wedding Vows

61   *Although Mrs. Spencer enjoyed*
      UNC Bicentennial, 10; Chamberlain, 99.

61   **President Swain paid no attention**
      Spencer Papers, Mrs. Spencer to Mrs. Swain, June 26, 1869.

61   *A widow who long mourned*
      Spencer, "Letter from," May 12, 1865; Chamberlain, 97.

62   *Mrs. Spencer had not been*
      Russell, 182; Chamberlain, 98; Spencer Papers.

62   *During the long summer days*
      Atkins, E.H.S., Unpublished, October 3, 1865.

62   *Back in Chapel Hill*
      Chamberlain, 98; Wiley, 145; Hague, 81; Spencer, *First Steps,* 209; McGuire,
      292. Many Southern women were forced to remake old dresses during the war
      because of textile shortages caused by blockades. The shortages continued for
      a few years after the war.

63   *The Swains sent few invitations*
      Chamberlain, 98–99; Spencer Papers, June 26, 1869; Russell, 70; Snider, 70.

63   *By all reports, Ella was*
      Barile.

63   *Attending the ceremony were*
      Chamberlain, 98; Graham, John W., letter to David Swain, June 11, 1866;
      Graham, *Papers,* Vol. 7, 143, 223, 260.

64   *Officiating was the Reverend*
      Atkins Bible (Eleanor H. and Smith D.); Chapel of the Cross Record Book;
      1789 U.S. Book of Common Prayer. Hubbard wrote in the church's Record
      Book: *Brig. General Smith D. Atkins, of Freeport, Illinois, to Miss Eleanor H.
      Swain, daughter of Governor D.S. Swain.* The marriage bond was posted with
      bondsman H.B. Guthrie on August 21, 1865.

64   *Even as Ella and the general*
      Chamberlain, 98; Atkins, E.H.S., Unpublished, November 1868, and
      December 3, 1868; "Marriages," *Weekly Record*; Swain, E.W., Unpublished,
      Mrs. Swain to Anne Swain, January 16, 1856; Brown, 17; Barile. Ella's wedding
      ring has been passed down through generations of her family: to her daughter,
      Eleanor Hope (Dot) Atkins Cobb, her granddaughter, Eleanor Hope Cobb

Newell, her great-granddaughter, Eleanor Hope (Wuff) Newell Maynard, and her great-great-granddaughter, Eleanor Hope Maynard, sister of the author.

65 *It was the wedding cake*
Russell, 69–70; Chapel of the Cross Record Book.

66 *In contrast, Illinois papers*
Freeport Journal, September 27, 1865.

67 *After the wedding, Mrs. Spencer*
Russell, 70; Spencer Papers, June 26, 1869.

67 *Outrage about the marriage*
UNC Bicentennial, 10; Jones, H.G., *North Carolina*, 263; Smith, 83; Spencer Papers; Wagstaff, 13. Jones concludes, "The University of North Carolina survived the war, but fell victim to partisan politics during Reconstruction. The effectiveness of David L. Swain, president since 1835, was compromised in the public eye when his daughter Eleanor married Smith D. Atkins, commanding general of the Union troops occupying Chapel Hill. . . . Her father's permission having been secured, Eleanor Hope Swain, against the protest of friends, married the Union General. . . . This marriage provoked much adverse criticism throughout the State. President Swain's course was censured by many, some being alienated from the University on account of it; but now that prejudice has yielded to reason, his wisdom in this matter is admitted. Had all been as charitable as he was, the wounds of the War would soon have been healed."

Mrs. Spencer wrote to Mrs. Swain June 26, 1869, "Prof. McIver was talking about it this spring. . . . He repeated to me as truths, which he had all along believed—some most ridiculous tales. I had the satisfaction of setting him right. I asked Dr. Hubbard about the propriety of writing about it & read him what I wrote. I was so afraid of saying too much. He approved very decidedly & said it was due to Governor Swain to say that much at least."

Wagstaff, a history professor at UNC, wrote in 1950 of the marriage: "Here was proof positive to Confederates bitter in defeat. . . . The marriage was made a *cause célèbre* . . . to denounce Swain and the University was proof of loyalty to the lost Southern cause."

CHAPTER SIX—The Wide-Awake Life

71 *At the end of August*
Chamberlain, 99; *Freeport Journal*, September 27, 1865, May 1, 1867; Graham,

Papers, Vol. 6, 63. The *Journal* reported, "Less than forty years ago the place where Freeport now stands was occupied by a small Indian village, under the command of the old Chief Winneshiek, and was first visited at that time by white men for trading. . . . In 1835, Wm. Baker built the first log cabin on the banks of the Pecatonica . . . and moved his family into this wilderness to live. He was followed, in 1836, by a number of others, among them O.H. Wright, who started a store. . . ."

71 *In Freeport, Ella felt a sense*
Russell, 12–13; Graham, *Papers,* Vol. 6, 63; "Preserving Chapel Hill's Past"; "Old Chapel Hill Cemetery"; *In the Footprints,* 20; *Freeport Journal,* September 27, 1865. The only grandparent Ella knew was her mother's mother, Anna Caswell White, who died in 1850 when Ella was eight. Her maternal grandfather, William White, died in 1811. Her father's mother, Caroline Swain, died on December 25, 1842, and her father's father, George Swain, died on December 24, 1829.
       Ella, Anne, and Bunkey enjoyed visiting their mother's sisters in Raleigh. Swain wrote Graham April 16, 1864, "Mrs. Swain and I are alone at home. The girls have been in Raleigh for the last three weeks."

71 *The couple initially lived*
Atkins, E.H.S., Unpublished letters; Carlile, "Brewster Boast"; *Freeport Journal.* The *Journal* reported, "Brewster House started in 1855 . . . four stories plus basement . . . bar, barber shop, bathing room, stone cellar, exchange office, dry good store, banking room, private entrance for ladies, servants rooms, dry room, laundry, gentleman's parlor, ladies private parlor, ladies parlor, dining hall, kitchen, pantry, pastry rooms, parlors w/bdrms. . . . The hotel itself is to be an elegant one, a credit and a source of profit, if well conducted, to the proprietor, the landlord and the city. . . . The public may rest assured that no pains will be spared . . . cost $55,000. . . . From the very beginning, the BH was recognized as the place to have balls and other social events. . . . [It] closed in 1932."

72 *Their quarters were on the third floor*
Carlile, "Brewster Boast"; Atkins, E.H.S., Unpublished letters; Culpepper, 207–08; Atkins Bible (Smith D.). Cynthia Krinbill was twenty years older than Smith. Her children were Sarah (born December 1, 1854), Carrie (born April 2, 1856), and Martin (born August 27, 1861). Culpepper notes that while affluent women of the Confederacy were "reveling in levity and luxury, most women were engaged in a four-year struggle with privation—with inflation and shortages that for some were merely annoyances but which for others assumed life-threatening dimensions."

73 *Happy as they were*
Freeport Journal, December 5, 1865; Carpenter, 82; Freedmen's; Oberholtzer, 128; Graham, *Papers,* Volume 6, 376–79; Atkins, Personal notes. On

October 1, 1865, North Carolina Freedmen Bureau Assistant Superintendent John C. Barnett explained, "Knowing that many of you have the wrong impressions relative to your freedom, I sent this circular ['Circular to the Freedmen'] that it may correct erroneous ideas. . . . The Government has given you your freedom, and you must not expect anything further from it. The Government expects you to labor and work out your own salvation; and, unless you do, you go back to slavery, or a condition far worse. . . . Any property that you possess hereafter, you must acquire by labor, industry, and honesty. At the end of the year, those who have remained with their former masters, and worked faithfully, will be paid liberally . . . able to provide clothing and food for themselves . . . for a portion of another year . . . and . . . if they have conducted themselves as to gain the confidence and respect of their employers, be able to retain their places for another year. . . . A long Winter is before you, and unless you provide for that time, your families must suffer—yea, many must perish. . . . Government will not feed any who . . . are able to work. You have had four months of freedom . . . your rights consist of your freedom . . . to make your own contracts, to receive the benefit of your own labor, to choose your own employer, to keep and govern your own families, to educate your children, and to worship God after your own manner. . . . As regards to your right to vote . . . you have other and more important matters to attend to now. Never agitate this question, but leave it for others to settle. In order to vote, a man should be educated. You are not. Had you that right in your present situation, it would be a curse to you . . . so dream not, talk not of things that . . . would be to your disadvantage and to your injury. . . . You must do for yourselves."

74 *Earning a living was important*
Freeport Journal, December 5, 1865.

75 *As Ella's pregnancy progressed*
O'Malley; Atkins Bible (Eleanor H. and Smith D.); *Freeport Journal*, March 12, 1913; Graham, *Papers*, Vol. 7, 143, 223, 260. Naming the baby for two men who had been kind to a Yankee general was General Atkins's tribute to them. The Grahams had dined with the Swains and Atkinses, and Atkins had volunteered to send Graham a copy of a speech by Illinois Senator Lyman Trumbull that mentioned Graham.

Ella's letters to her family often ended with "write me as often as you can," "your child in love," "your own child," and "blessings from your child."

75 *Shortly after their first wedding anniversary*
Atkins Bible (Eleanor H. and Smith D.); Chamberlain, 131–33.

75 *The intervening year had not been*
Powell, *The First*, 89–90; Battle, *History*, Vol. 1, 752–55; Leloudis, "Civil War"; Chamberlain, 133; Russell, 82, 83.

76   *Ella and the general's first trip*
Chamberlain, 132; Battle, *History*, Vol. 1, 751–52.

77   *Ella didn't seem to notice*
Atkins, E.H., Unpublished letters, February 1, 1868; Barile; Goldsmith.

CHAPTER SEVEN — Anne

81   *In early winter of 1867*
Graham, *Papers*, Vol. 7, 124, 155, 233, 252, 290, 296; Barile. Swain wrote
Graham on November 9, 1866, that Atkins was preparing to leave for Freeport.
Ella and her mother were leaving for Raleigh to visit White Hall when "Ella
was taken quite ill, and has been in bed ever since. I hope she is out of danger
now." On November 31, he noted she was "improving in health, & will, I hope,
be able to leave her room in two or three days."

82   *Anne was two years old*
Swain Bible; National Governors; Swain, Manuscripts; Murray, 207; Waugh,
29; Battle, *History*, 423–24; Chamberlain, 54; Swain, E.W., Unpublished;
Barile; Ivey, "Town & Gown," 1. The Governor's Palace was located on present
site of Meymandi Hall and Memorial Auditorium. During Swain's tenure as
governor, the family shared quarters with the state legislature after a June 1831
fire destroyed the Capitol, referred to as the Statehouse.

84   *Anne also suffered from chronic*
Ivey, "Town & Gown," 1; Brecher; Barile.

85   *That her final suffering*
Graham, *Papers*, Vol. 7, 290, 297; Swain, Manuscripts; Spencer Papers, David
Swain to Mrs. Spencer, August 24, 1867.

86   *During her funeral held two days*
Swain Bible; Russell, 24; Chapel of the Cross Record Book.

CHAPTER EIGHT — Life on Prospect Terrace

89 *Smith Atkins, who had traveled*
Atkins Bible (Eleanor H. and Smith D.); Graham, *Papers*, Vol. 7, 330. Swain wrote Graham that Mrs. Swain was distraught over Anne's death, noting on June 1, "Eleanor seems to be inconsolable" because of the "melancholy event."

89 *When the Atkins family*
Atkins, E.H.S., Unpublished, November 6, 1867, December 3, 1867, February 8 and 9, 1868, March 1, 1868, March 23, 1868, March 27, 1868.

90 *General Atkins had a lot to balance*
Freeport Journal, May 1, 1867, January 8, 1868. Atkins submitted a monument design that was accepted. It was eighty-three feet high with a statue of Victory on top. The *Journal* noted, "The last great work of this artist [Giovanni Meli] . . . from an original design, which is intended to render in terra cotta . . . being thirteen feet high. It is, even to the minute detail, finished as perfectly as the finest marble statue."

90 *With a baby and a new*
Atkins, E.H.S., Unpublished, February 9, 1868, March 1, 1868, March 23, 1868; Atkins, Personal Journal, December 4 and 5, 1854.

93 *For Bunkey, it had been*
Barile; Battle, *History*, Vol. 1, 810; Vance, *Papers*, Vol. 1, 4; Wagner; *Catalogue of*; Guernsey and Alden, 14, 61; Cobb Loan, George Swain to David Swain, April 26, 1822, May 3, 1822, May 10, 1822, May 31, 1822, June 7, 1822, June 21, 1822, July 19, 1822, and David Swain to George Swain, April 24, 1822, April 25, 1822, May 2, 1822, May 18, 1822, June 18, 1822, July 6, 1822, July 19, 1822, July 21, 1822, August 2, 1822; Arthur, 404. Prior to enrolling at Jefferson Medical College, Bunkey visited his Swain relatives in Asheville. Family friend and former Governor Vance saw him there and assured the elder Swain, "Richard is looking very well."

Bunkey entered university in June 1852; by the end of his first year he was having trouble with his studies and, it seems, his behavior. Aunt Susan tried to convince him to stay in school, recounting difficulties and death at age twenty-one of a family friend: "William was not as strong as his father wished his son to be, his associates were not such as his father liked. . . . I call your attention to his death, just to restate to you the course he pursued the latter part of his life, and the reason I have for this is an expression I heard you use when here last. 'I shall in six years be 21, then I will be free and will do as I please.'"

Her November 13, 1853, words appear to have gone unheeded; Bunkey announced he might drop out and attend another college. Yet he sought the

advice of all his aunts, and received an earful from Betsy: "Take the coun-
sel and advice of your father who loves you and takes more interest in you
than any human being can except your devoted mother. His judgment is far
superior to yours, and if you could have an idea of the solitude and anxiety of
parents for the welfare of their children your good sense would teach you and
the natural affections of your heart would lead you to submit cheerfully to the
wishes of those parents." She described his parents "who have watched over
you in helpless infancy, taken the great care of you and promised themselves
a rich reward in having a son to be an honor to them in their old age and
a consolation when about to leave the world. . . . Crush not the hopes of
your Father, trouble not the heart of your Mother. . . . resolve never again
to be guilty of improper conduct but strive to be all as far as you are capable
of being."

Aunt Susan wrote that same week, suggesting he "be willing to be set right
by those that have experience." Warning that he would encounter "many trials
and temptations" and should not "think your case is different from others," she
explained that "boys are more exposed to temptation than girls, but all have to
be on their guard."

The aunts' interest in his well-being was finally rewarded when he returned
to school—and to the university. Susan wrote him August 14, 1854: "I was
much pleased to find you thought to write me. And more pleased to find you
had entered college with such good resolutions to do well. . . . let nothing
break that good resolution of staying at home, studying your books." To be
successful, she advised, "test your talents if they have been dormant. . . . keep
to this good resolution, be diligent, and you will thereby be able to make your
father's heart glad."

Eleanor Swain seemed particularly pleased with her son's decision, noting
in a January 16, 1856, letter to Anne, "Bunk is fixing up the office for the reception of his friend and room mate Mason. . . . It has been doubtful for three
months whether Bunk would go back to college, but I believe he intends to
continue now." She wished "some good spirit would hover around my Bunkey
too and inspire him to action wanting of the gifts and talent committed to
him by his great creator."

President Swain might not have been surprised by his son's reluctance to
pursue his education—as a first-year university student in 1822, and the first
boy to enter state university from the west (according to historian John Preston Arthur), he wanted to quit after four months, asking his father on April 24,
1822, not to be angry: "I ask no pardon for troubling you with a minute detail
of all the circumstances which have befallen me, since I left Salisbury up to
which date my letter from that place has furnished a full account of myself."
He had been advised that if he read law with John Louis Taylor, North Carolina Supreme Court Chief Justice, and attended lectures until commencement
and "continue[d] with him for 12 months from the character given him, of me
by Mr. Gales, he has no doubt but that he can in that length of time of his
prepare me" for a career in law (April 20, 1822).

Initially concerned, George Swain finally agreed (July 19, 1822): "I don't however blame you for changing your mind in that respect after having time to read your letter leisurely, and weigh your arguments." His mother, Caroline, wrote (August 23, 1822), "My only care for you is your future welfare."

94 *President Swain, however, had a job*

White, Last Will; "N.C. Revolutionary"; Lea, 52–67. The property originally had been given to William White, Bunkey's maternal grandfather, in lieu of payment for his service to the United States during the Revolutionary War. It had since been divided between Bunkey's mother and her sisters.

94 *Bunkey did more than check*

Swain Bible; Swain, E.W., Unpublished, February 4, 1862; Spencer Papers, April 6, 1862; *North Carolina Standard; Freeport Journal*, February 2, 1872; Barile. Bunkey's cousin Gartha Ann Barringer Blakemore and her husband, J.W. Blakemore, were witnesses. Gartha was Aunt Nancy's daughter.

94 *Grief-stricken, Bunkey left*

"History of the 39th." Coleman was the son of David Swain's sister, Cynthia.

94 *As an assistant surgeon*

Phillips, *Best Foot*; "History of the 39th"; Swain Bible.

95 *As the war continued*

Atkins, E.H.S., Unpublished, November 6, 1867; Graham, *Papers,* Vol. 7, 287; Swain, E.W., Unpublished, November 18, 1865. After her brother set up his practice in Shannon, Ella wrote her parents, "Bunk . . . was looking very well & still promises to do the best he can & that will be well if he only half tries."

95 *In her letters home, Ella*

Atkins, E.H.S., Unpublished, February 9, 1868, March 1, 1868. In her February 9 letter, Ella also addressed Bunkey's drinking: "I am so pleased to tell you that we hear the very best accounts of Bunk since Christmas he has been perfectly sober & industrious has not even left his business to come to see us but twice & he seems more steady in his purpose by his conversation & letters than I ever knew him to or thought it possible for him to be."

96 *That Friday evening, Ella*

Atkins, E.H.S., Unpublished, March 1, 1868, December 3, 1868.

97 *Ella's correspondence was newsy*

Atkins, E.H.S., Unpublished, February 9, 1868, March 1, 1868, November 1868, December 3, 1868; Lefler and Stanford, 333; Fulwider, 571. According to Lefler and Stanford, feelings toward Johnson "were mixed, for while he was Southern-born and bred and wanted what was best for the South at war's end, Radicals in the North were not as conciliatory. In North Carolina, the result of the Reconstruction Act was felt with military rule, the denial of voting rights for some whites, voting rights for blacks, and readmission to the Union only after a Republican governor and legislature were elected to follow the desires of the Radicals.

Fulwider adds, "An attempt to have Mr. Atkins removed because he was a follower of the Andrew Johnson faction failed. The General continued to hold office under General Grant's Presidency, and it was said that he was the only postmaster who remained under Grant that had served during Johnson's term. General Atkins continued to hold the office under Hayes, Garfield and Arthur.

"The election of Cleveland in 1884 and again in 1892, caused the appointment of [a] Democrat and Mr. John F. Smith served from 1885 to 1889, and F. Charles Donohue from 1893 to 1897. From 1889 to 1893, during Harrison's term, General Atkins was again postmaster and in 1897, after the election of McKinley he was again appointed and has since held the position by appointment under President Roosevelt and President Taft."

98 *Marriage and motherhood*
Atkins, E.H.S., Unpublished, March 1, 1868, March 27, 1868; Russell, 24. Fourteen years later, in a January 24, 1881, letter to Emma White, Mrs. Spencer wrote of Anne's death: "No hyacinths will ever again be as sweet to me as those early white ones Anne used to bring us from your garden in February long ago."

CHAPTER NINE — My Desolate Home

101 *Though she still mourned Anne*
Atkins, E.H.S., Unpublished, March 23, 1868, March 27, 1868, March 29, 1868.

101 *Thus it came as a deep shock*
Atkins, E.H.S., Unpublished, July 10, 1868; Atkins Bible (Eleanor H. and Smith D); "Second Summer," 181.

102 *"My Desolate Home"*
Atkins, E.H.S., Unpublished, "My Desolate Home," and July 10, 1868.

106 *In mid-August, Ella and Genl*
Atkins, E.H.S., Unpublished, August 23, 1868; Russell, 103; Phillips, *North Carolina Presbyterian*; *Freeport Journal*, September 2, 1868; Spencer, "Proceedings" and "The Late"; Spencer Papers, letter to E.W. Swain, August 7, 1882.

106 **For more than three decades**

Battle, *History,* Vol. 1, 754–57, 774–80; Spencer, "Proceedings," 54; Graham, *Papers,* Vol. 6, 83; Russell, 103; "Confederate Army"; Downs, "Historical Sketch"; Phillips, *North Carolina Presbyterian*; Atkins, E.H.S., Unpublished, August 23, 1868; *Freeport Journal,* September 2, 1868. Mrs. Spencer wrote that when the accident occurred Swain had been planning a trip to "his native mountains in Buncombe" with the hope "to restore tone to body and mind before taking final leave of Chapel Hill."

Battle notes, "This venerable man, full of years and honors, who had held high places in the executive, legislative and judicial departments of the State, who for over one-third of a century had charge of its chief institution of learning, who had influenced for good thousands of the leaders of the people in public and private life, so saturated with love of the University that he sought to control her even in her desolation, under new and untried guardians, but by them coldly and without explanation turned away."

Swain's dedication is clear in a letter to Graham (January 20, 1862): "Your letter . . . finds me, as it left you, just rising from a bed of sickness. I have been quite ill—since the evening of the 1ˢᵗ. I have heard my class in my bed chamber this morning, nevertheless, and am to hear them again this evening."

Years later he wrote Graham (April 16, 1864) that the "military bill threatens our existence," and (on May 3) "I had intended to reply before you left home, but have been constantly engaged in efforts to preserve life in the University." He was referring to the Third Conscription Act of February 1864 that made all able-bodied white men between the ages of seventeen and fifty eligible for the draft, an act that would threaten the already diminished numbers of UNC students and faculty.

In her 1869 Swain biography, Mrs. Spencer explained of the Landscript, "From this important aid to the shattered finances of the Institution, he hoped great things." Battle notes on July 30, 1867, Swain offered his resignation as president in a letter to the Board of Trustees, "at the earliest period at which the Board may be pleased to designate a successor."

110 **The obituary Mrs. Spencer wrote**

Spencer, *North Carolina Presbyterian.*

110 **Mrs. Spencer believed President Swain's**

Russell, 103; Spencer Papers, August 7 and August 27, 1882; Spencer, "The Late"; Daniels, June 7, 1889.

CHAPTER TEN — Moving On

115 *After President Swain's funeral*
Atkins, E.H.S., Unpublished, October 6, 1868.

116 *When Mrs. Swain did not respond*
Atkins, E.H.S., Unpublished, November 1868.

116 *Over the years, Genl had*
Atkins, E.H.S., Unpublished, November 1868; Burns.

118 *Mrs. Swain finally wrote*
Atkins, E.H.S., Unpublished, November 1868; Graham, *Papers,* Vol. 7, 639;
Battle, *History,* Vol. 1, 780, and Vol. 2, 345; Public Laws; Murray, 587–89;
Historic Oakwood; Russell, 130; Chamberlain, 176–77, 181; Wise, 111–12;
Barile. Mrs. Swain was close to her sisters. From 1846–1849, they worked on
a quilt, despite Nancy living in Tennessee and Betsy in La Grange, North
Carolina. The quilt, stitched with family names and Bible verses, was donated
by Eleanor Swain's descendents to the North Carolina Museum of History.
On January 1, 1857, Sophronia, Emma, and Susan signed agreement to share
the Raleigh house. They covenanted to "live together at the family mansion in
Raleigh upon the following terms and conditions. . . . They will keep on their
lots in Raleigh & in the family plantation in Wake County, so many of the
slaves belonging to each one of them, so they shall deem necessary for their
comfort. . . . All necessary expenses of the mansion house & plantation shall
be a common charge, to be borne equally by all the parties." Emma was to
receive all money, keep "a regular book of entries of all her transactions,
as well in the way of receipts and disbursements," and at the end of each year
"exhibit and render to the other parties—a just & full account of the same."
Any surplus was to be divided equally. On June 5, 1857, Sophronia deeded her
interest in lots 158 and 159 to Susan and Emma.
There is no record of Mrs. Swain signing an agreement with them when
she moved to Raleigh in late 1868 following her husband's death. In March
1872, Mrs. Spencer wrote, "it is very unusual to see so large a family of sisters
together so late in life."
The land on which Raleigh's Oakwood Cemetery was established was
adjacent to the Confederate Cemetery opened in February 1867 after the state's
Reconstruction government declared that four hundred graves of Confederate
soldiers in the Rock Quarry Cemetery had to be moved.
Graham notes in a December 11, 1868, letter to his wife, "Mrs. Swain had
returned to Raleigh. But I did not see them at Miss Whites." Mrs. Spencer's
letter to Mrs. Swain of December 16, 1869, notes that the graves had been
moved in mid-December. Susan White was one of the incorporators of
the cemetery.

In December 1869, Mrs. Spencer congratulated her on "having your dead together, and near you. I did hope, that the time would come within a year or two that you would feel willing to let the remains of your beloved and honored husband remain here where his life work was done. But of late the signs are evident of no sense of gratitude, or even of decent remembrance and respect."

119 *As comforting as she tried to be*
Atkins, E.H.S., Unpublished, December 8, 1868.

120 *Rest was necessary because Ella*
Atkins, E.H.S., Unpublished, November 1868; Atkins Bible (Eleanor H. and Smith D.); *Freeport Journal*, October 28, 1868. Captain Cockley and his wife were unable to meet the Atkinses in Chicago.

121 *With a new year*
Bulletin, June 2, 1869; *Freeport Journal*, October 20, 1869.

122 *Ella spent early 1869*
Barile; Atkins Bible (Eleanor H. and Smith D.).

122 *Now a mother for the third time*
Atkins Bible (Eleanor H. and Smith D.); United States, Census.

122 *Their emotional support was*
Freeport Journal, August 11, 1869.

122 *Four months later, Sarah Atkins*
Atkins Bible (Eleanor H. and Smith D.); *Freeport Journal*, December 28, 1869. Mrs. Atkins died December 18, 1869.

123 *To cope with his grief*
Freeport Journal, October 8, 1869. The elder Atkinses moved from Ella and Genl's home to the home of their daughter, Cynthia Krinbill, and her family in late 1868.

123 *Ella, on the other hand*
Russell, 136; *Freeport Journal*, December 28, 1870; Graham, *Papers*, Vol. 8, 233; United States, Census; Spencer Papers, December 21, 1871.

124 *Although never a regular churchgoer*
Battle, *History*, Vol. 1, 535; Swain, E.W., Unpublished, February 4, 1862; Barile. According to Battle, Mrs. Swain did not attend church regularly, but the many religious events for her children took place at the nearby Episcopal church; her husband was an elder and a founding member of Chapel Hill's Presbyterian church; she and her husband were married by Presbyterian minister William McPheeters. Her faith clearly was strong.

124 *Instinctively, the Atkinses relied*
Freeport Journal, February 7, 1872; Atkins, E.H.S., Unpublished, July 10, 1868; Spencer Papers, Charles Phillips to Mrs. Swain, February 16, 1872, and Mrs. Spencer to Mrs. Swain, March 13, 1872; Swain Bible. Mrs. Spencer wrote that she had heard Bunkey was ill, "which was, it seems, indirectly as much the cause of his death as if he had died in bed." She did not elaborate.

126 *Also keeping her in Illinois*
Atkins Bible (Eleanor H. and Smith D.); Spencer Papers. After Dyke was born in November 1872, Mrs. Spencer wrote Mrs. Swain in Freeport January 31, 1873: "Give my love to Ellie & a kiss to each of her babies. I am glad she has two."

126 *Meanwhile, the newly widowed Maggie*
Barile; Spencer Papers; "Funeral Services" and "In the Haven," *Asheville Daily Citizen*; "Former Resident," *Sunday Citizen*; "Mrs. Clayton," *Asheville Times*; Parish Register 1890–1900; Green, 12–13, 36, 103; *City Directory*; Historic Riverside Cemetery, 56; Digges, *Buncombe County . . . Grantee* and *Buncombe County . . . Grantor*; Register of Deeds; United States, Census. Maggie's father, Volney Steele, died in 1870. When Maggie left for Tennessee, she apparently was pregnant with her and Bunkey's second child. Mrs. Spencer asked in an August 21, 1872, letter if Mrs. Swain had news of Maggie and Lula, and wondered, "Did she ever have the so long expected addition?" Maggie's obituary noted she was pre-deceased by a son who died at sixteen months (no record of his birth or death is in Swain Bible). On August 17, 1875, Maggie married Bailey (also Balie and Baylie) Peyton "Dick" Steele, her cousin who served with Company B of Field's Tennessee Infantry during the Civil War and was employed as a railroad engineer. Lucy C. Steele was born in 1880, and another girl, Willie Warder (Wil-Warder), in 1882.

   After Bunkey's death, Lula lived with her mother and grandmother, then with her mother, stepfather, and half-sisters in Shelbyville and Tullahoma, Tennessee. At twenty-five, the age of majority for women, she went to Asheville to see the land her paternal grandmother, Mrs. Swain, had left her. Lula's great-grandfather, George Edward Swain, purchased large tracts around Morristown (renamed Asheville) in the late 1780s through the early 1800s, though most were sold before he died. His son, David Lowry Swain, bought some of his land, as well as additional tracts, some of which he sold while university president. After he died, Mrs. Swain periodically sold land, presumably to help support the Raleigh household she shared with her sisters. When she died in 1883, some land was sold to cover her estate debts. The rest of the Buncombe County property went to Lula.

   In January and March 1888, according to Buncombe County Deeds, Lula sold 200 acres on the north fork of Swannanoa River, property on Black Mountain, and 600 acres in Bee Tree Creek. In May, she purchased a tract in

Flat Creek, north of Asheville. About that time, she met local druggist, James S. Grant, a Scotsman whose business was in the 24 S. Main Street building once owned by Lula's great-grandfather, George Swain. She must have been swept her off her feet; they married on October 17, 1889, in Tullahoma, Tennessee, then returned to Asheville. They sold Flat Creek property weeks before Margaret Louise Swain Grant was born on June 30, 1890.

In 1891–92, Maggie, Dick, and daughters Wil-Warder and Lucy moved to Asheville to be closer to Lula and granddaughter/niece Margaret Louise. Lula gave birth to a son in November 1892. He was baptized James Swain Grant on October 21, 1893, at home by Charles T. Quintard, the Bishop of Tennessee. The baby's step-grandfather and Aunt Lucy were his sponsors, according to Trinity Episcopal Church records.

The Grant marriage fell apart the next year; they sold their home in February 1894. A year later, and three years after moving to Asheville to be closer to her eldest daughter and grandchildren, Maggie died at fifty-one, having suffered "a painful illness of four months, which she bore with her native fortitude of character, coupled with that beautiful and trusting Christian faith and resignation which faces death without a fear." She was buried in Asheville's Riverside Cemetery. Steele moved back to Tennessee, apparently leaving thirteen-year-old Wil-Warder with Lula; no record of where Lucy, then eighteen, lived. By 1896, Lula and her children lived at 99 College Street; she had hired a manager for the drugstore, which she bought from her former husband May 11, 1895.

The 1896 Asheville *City Directory* listed Lula as *Mrs.* By the 1899 census, she had moved to 63 Charlotte Street and was listed as *Miss.* Next references to her marital status in the 1900 Asheville *City Directory* list her as *widow of J.S. Grant*; in the 1900 census, she is listed as *divorced and proprietor of Grant's Drugstore.* Margaret was nine and David, called "Swain," was seven.

While running the business, Lula also cared for a sick child: Margaret contracted amoebic dysentery and died on June 29, 1901, a day before her twelfth birthday. Her death certificate lists her burial in Riverside Cemetery near her grandparents, but there is no cemetery record or marker.

In the Bible she had given Margaret the previous Christmas, Lula now wrote, *Margaret Grant, only daughter of Mrs. Louise Swain Grant (died June 29, 1901—the day before her 12th birthday).*

Two years later, on June 2, 1903, Lula married Thaddeus E. Clayton, grandson of Colonel Ephraim Clayton, well-known carpenter and manufacturer of rifles made from Cranberry Mines iron during the Civil War. He was also the great-grandson of Revolutionary War hero Lambert Clayton, who fought at King's Mountain, Guilford Courthouse, and Eutaw Springs. On April 27, 1904, Louise Swain was born, named for her deceased older sister; on November 25, 1906, Emma (later renamed Eleanor Swain), joined the family.

The census did not list Wil-Warder as living with Lula during those years. Dick Steele, retired, was living in a Tullahoma boarding house when he died

July 8, 1911. The *Asheville Daily Citizen* ("Former Resident Dies in Tennessee") reported he was "in several of the most famous battles" of Civil War and "received a wound that gave him more or less trouble until death." Wil-Warder had traveled to Tullahoma when she heard her father was ill, but arrived after he died. She brought his body back to Asheville. He was buried beside his wife in Riverside Cemetery.

Lucy married W.T. Kirk before her father's death and had daughters Westray in 1906 and Peyton in 1912. Both married; only Westray, who died in 1987, had children. Lucy died in 1959. Peyton celebrated her ninety-seventh birthday and died in 2009 at her New York City home. Wil-Warder is listed in the 1910 census as a public schoolteacher in Greensboro, North Carolina.

What James Grant did to cause Lula to divorce him was enough for her to change her son's first name—James Swain Grant became David Swain Grant. The first mention of the change was in the 1912 Asheville *City Directory: David S. Grant, student.* In census documents after his mother married Clayton, he is listed as *David S. Clayton.* In World War I, he enlisted as *David Swain Grant,* serving in the US Army's Thirty-ninth Infantry Regiment, Fourth Infantry Division. His grandfather Bunkey Swain had served in the Thirty-ninth North Carolina during the Civil War. David achieved rank of Second Lieutenant. He was killed in action August 5, 1918, and buried at Aisne-Marne American Cemetery in Belleau, France. The twenty-five-year-old was posthumously awarded the Distinguished Service Cross and French Croix de Guerre.

Lula again wrote in her Bible: *Margaret's splendid big brother has joined her. Bless my children.* Flowers are pressed between the pages and a note of "songs to sing over my dead body."

The 1915 Asheville *City Directory* listed Thad Clayton as employed with Miller-Clayton Paint Company. Clayton suffered a cerebral hemorrhage in 1935, and again on April 21, 1941. He died ten days later. He was seventy-eight.

Lula outlived her husband by six years and lived in an apartment in the Langren Hotel in Asheville. On September 12, 1947, eighty-year-old Lula was hit by a car as she stepped off the curb. She died of her injuries. She was buried in Riverside. Her grandson, Rod Speer, said David Swain Grant's battle awards were buried with her.

127 *As the writings of Mrs. Spencer*
Spencer Papers; Atkins, E.H.S., Unpublished, March 1, 1868, and November 1868; Atkins, Personal Journal; Atkins Bible (Eleanor H. and Smith D.); *Freeport Journal,* November 24, 1875. Winters in Freeport, near southern Wisconsin, were harsh. Atkins wrote in his journal on February 1, 1855, "Today we have mail for the first time in a long while. This snowstorm the most severe of any within my recollection has almost entirely cut us off from any communication with the world without. It is so badly drifted that the railroads are completely blockaded and it is said that the drifts on the Rock Island road are 40 feet

deep." On Thanksgiving 1875, the *Freeport Journal* reported, "Two inches of snow fell on Sunday night, giving the little ones in the city a taste of their winter's sport."

128 *With his family in the South*
Freeport Journal, April 14, 1875. At the second annual fire department banquet, Atkins "highly commended the past record of the Firemen of Freeport." At the January 1875 meeting of Freeport Lyceum, on the topic of "Compulsory education in the rudimentary branches," he argued "eloquently of the cruelty of the measures, and the impossibility of enforcing it in places like Five Points of New York City. . . ." He was to argue in the affirmative at the February 5 meeting on the question of whether "planets are inhabited."

Atkins sold his interest in the *Freeport Journal*, investing in another paper, the *Budget*, when it moved from Davis, Illinois, to Freeport. He remained active in politics, serving on the 1874 Republican Congressional Convention committee held in Freeport, speaking at rallies, and assisting with Ninety-second Illinois reunions. When Freeport's Public Library was established in space donated by the YMCA, Atkins served as the first president of its board.

128 *No sooner had he shed that*
Atkins Bible (Eleanor H. and Smith D.); Swain Bible.

CHAPTER ELEVEN — Ella

131 *All the while, Mrs. Spencer*
Spencer Papers, January 17, 1869, and June 26, 1869; Chamberlain, 155, 161, 168, 175, 226–27; Russell, 159; Battle, *History*, Vol. 2, 130–31; Daniels, "University Centennial," *Raleigh State Chronicle*. Mrs. Spencer asked Eleanor Swain for assistance in providing biographical information for the article she was writing on President Swain, which discussed how North Carolinians had felt about Ella's wedding. She offered to help Mrs. Swain with any task in Chapel Hill and to pick up a book that had belonged to David Swain.

Mrs. Spencer wrote January 31, 1873, "Your letters—allow me to say—are such elegant specimens of epistolary composition, & exhibit you in so new a light to some who have known you longest that I cannot help showing them now & then to such old friends." Her November 30, 1876, letter notes, "This is Thanksgiving day. I hope you & E. have enjoyed it together. . . ." She wrote on January 31, 1877, "None of us had heard from you, or of you in a long time, & we were all getting anxious to know if you were in your usual health—& I, for my part, was getting afraid you had become more indifferent to your old friends hereabouts."

She wrote Emma White on January 24, 1881, that she thought of Mrs. Swain on her wedding anniversary and on President Swain's birthday, but "she ceased to reply to my letters." On January 30, 1881, she wrote, "I really long to know something of you. . . ." On January 30, 1882, she wrote, "I do not hear anything of you or from you these days, but as long as you live & I live, I shall write to you every now & then."

Mrs. Swain provided some assistance to former neighbors-in-need. Mrs. Spencer detailed how she spent $20 Mrs. Swain had sent: "Two days before I got your letter, old aunt Milly W. came to ask me to write to you for her & beg for a little help. She is quite crippled with rheumatism & unable to work—even if she cd get work. I promised her I wd write—but your letter came before I found the time. I sent the poor old soul her $5.00. . . . She clapped her hands, & cried out 'I knowed Miss Eleanor would—I knowed she would'—I sent Emeline 3.00 & her supply of paper & envelopes & a new pen, & have a bottle of ink for her—so that I hope she will find it easy to write. . . . I went . . . to see Mrs. Eliza Hunt & take her a portion of your bounty. She was really affected on receiving it, & told me to tell you the thought that you remembered her way off yonder, did her most as much good as the money. . . . I sent Miss Fanny Yancey $2.00. . . . I gave old Mr. Elkins $2.50."

132 *A year later, certain the*
Battle, *History*, Vol. 2, 135; Spencer Papers, February 1877. A year after the university reopened, the Executive Committee of the Board of Trustees established October 12 as a "perpetual holiday to commemorate the laying of the corner stone of the Old East Building in 1793."

132 *Whether David Swain's grandson*
Atkins Bible (Eleanor H. and Smith D.); Swain Bible; Barile. Peg Isaac wrote on August 27, 1999, "I'm sure my grandmother was named for Susan White [Mrs. Swain's sister] and Sister Anne [Ella's sister]. I think my 'granny,' as I always called her, mentioned something about not liking 'Annie'—and probably just chose to use Anne. Sounds like her."

132 *A good and loving mother*
Barile.

134 *Suddenly, everything changed*
Freeport Bulletin, June 14, 1881; Barile; *Raleigh Sentinel*, n.d.; Newell.

136 *As a friend, Ella had*
Atkins, E.H.S., Unpublished, November 6, 1867, February 9, 1868, March 23, 1868, and December 3, 1868.

137 *Ella believed Southern ill-will*
Atkins, E.H.S., Unpublished, March 13, 1872; Spencer Papers, March 26, 1878. Mrs. Spencer's letter ends, "Ma begs her best love & remembrance to you & to your sisters—& include Ella in all."

137 *Upon learning of Ella's death*
Spencer Papers, June 23, 1881.

137 *Mrs. Swain now had lost*
Spencer Papers, August 26, 1881.

138 *Ella had once assured her mother*
Atkins, E.H., Unpublished, July 10, 1868.

CHAPTER TWELVE — Legacies

141 *After Ella's death, the bond*
Newell; Spencer Papers, August 26, 1881, January 30, 1882, August 27, 1882; Barile. That winter, Atkins traveled to Washington, DC, noted Mrs. Spencer (January 30, 1881): "I did not see him, but bro' S. [Sam] did."

141 *Their presence also helped*
Spencer Papers, October 9, 1882. Mrs. Spencer wrote, "I have thought of you so often since the tidings came that Miss Emma White had got her summons, & was gone over the river. One after another it seems to be your lot to see your loved ones go. One after another, you go down to the brink with them, & stand by them to the last. It is a blessed privilege, though heartbreaking. . . . I did not think when I saw your sisters in June, that Miss Emma would be the first to go. Miss Susan seemed so much the elder, & most feeble. . . ."

A letter about Susan's death followed on November 2, 1882: "I thank you very much for having made the exertion—painful as it must have been—to write me an account of dear Miss Susan's departure. . . . My earliest recollections of Anne are connected with 'Aunt Susan' of whom she loved to talk as a child, & to whom, in later years she used to quote constantly. The Governor too quoted her opinions a great deal. I have heard him speak of her judgment as almost infallible. He said once he knew few men whose advice he would take than hers in any affair of importance. He often expressed the highest esteem for her sense, integrity, & insight."

At the time of Mrs. Swain's death, her only living sibling, Betsy Felton, then widowed, was living at White Hall. Betsy died on July 5, 1883, five months after Eleanor's death.

142 *With her grandchildren there*
Battle, *History*, Vol. 2, 106–07; Jones, *For History's*, 239–56; Jones, J.S., "Historical." According to Battle, if Swain had lived, "he would have done what was right" for "he never claimed the papers as his own."

146 *Whether Ella or General Atkins*
Mintz, "Digital"; Spencer Papers, January 31, 1877; *Freeport Journal*, June 27, 1877; Atkins, "Decoration."

148 *Ella had never stopped trying*
Atkins, E.H.S., Unpublished, November 6, 1867, August 23, 1868, November 1868.

148 *She found an ally*
Atkins, E.H.S., Unpublished, February 9, 1868.

148 *Occasionally she chided her mother*
Atkins, E.H.S., Unpublished, November 1868.

148 *Despite her cool demeanor*
Spencer Papers, March 10, 1866.

150 *However, Mrs. Swain continued*
Jones, H.G., *For History's*, 253. Mrs. Swain wrote to Mrs. Spencer on September 2, 1875, "The reason for my connecting the debt due Mr. Swain from the Univ. with his history, was simply I regarded the Univ. & Historical Soc. as Institutions of the State, & I saw no justice in adding one obligation to another, when considering the probable loss in one case, & the value of the other."

151 *The controversy over the Swain*
Jones, H.G., *For History's*, 258–60; Spencer Papers, August 7, 1882; Swain, E.W., "Last Will."

151 *A month later, on February 5*
Barile; Swain Bible; *Journal and Republican*, February 17, 1883.

152 *Listed among the assets*
Swain, E.W., "Last Will"; Barile; Meeting of the Executive Committee; *Journal of the Senate of the General Assembly*, 430, 446, 600, 606, 631, 670; *Journal of the House of Representatives of the General Assembly*, 295, 297, 741, 897, 967; *Public Laws & Resolutions*, 1127–28; *Southeastern Reporter*, Vol. 64, 505–06. The marker in the Freeport City Cemetery was damaged in the 1930s and later replaced by the family. EHWS are Mrs. Swain's initials: Eleanor Hope White Swain.
    The debt to President Swain was finally paid, but not before the state Supreme Court so ordered. In March 1908, the UNC Board of Trustees Executive Committee was asked to repay the debt of $16,463.13, including interest, but financially it wasn't able to do so and turned the matter over to the General Assembly. A year later, on March 8, 1909, it passed an act "to compromise, adjust and settle the indebtedness of the University to the

estate of the late Governor David L. Swain." The $3,500 value given each of the individual bonds held by the estate was a compromise from an original estimate of $12,000 each. Mrs. Swain's executor, Walter Clark Jr., told the General Assembly that the heirs were willing to accept the lesser value and hoped the matter would be "put thru as soon as possible."

State Treasurer B.R. Lacy claimed the act directing the payment was not passed "in accordance with article 2, section 16 of the [state] Constitution," and declined to make the payment. The case went to Wake County Superior Court, which ruled in favor of the General Assembly's action. Lacy filed an appeal with the state Supreme Court, where Judge George H. Brown wrote the decision affirming the lower court's judgment.

Listed as the recipients were "the two surviving granddaughters"—Dot Atkins Cobb and Susie Atkins Rackley. Although Lula Swain was listed in Mrs. Swain's will, she was not listed as a recipient in the settlement. Dot and Susie may not have known that she had married and was living in Asheville in 1909.

CHAPTER THIRTEEN — The General

155 *Mrs. Swain's death left*
Atkins Bible (Eleanor H. and Smith D.); Carlile, "Newspapers in Freeport"; *Freeport Journal*, October 28, 1885.

155 *Little did he know*
Atkins Bible (Eleanor H. and Smith D).

155 *The general was devastated*
Freeport Journal, October 28, 1885; Russell, 182–83.

156 *Having lost his wife*
Barile; Isaac; Williams, *Diary,* 1; *Freeport Journal.* That same year, Atkins's sister, Cynthia Krinbill, with whom he and Ella had lived early in their marriage, died October 3. Atkins had also lost other family members—his brother, Louis, died December 17, 1882, at age forty-three, and his brother-in-law, Martin Krinbill, died in February 1884.

156 *As the years passed*
Freeport Journal, March 18, 1913; Atkins, Personal Journal, October 2, 1854, and February 17, 1855. Atkins grew more active politically; he was a candidate for the Republican nomination for Illinois State Treasurer in April 1894.

In campaign literature, he was described as "an active campaigner, a lucid speaker, a clean and convincing writer, a representative, a soldier and a man who, if nominated and elected State Treasurer, will make an efficient, honest official." He did not win nomination.

159 *Perhaps General Atkins, himself*
Committee, 247; Carpenter, "General Atkins," 84. Historian Carpenter noted in his memorial to Atkins, "It has seldom been the writer's lot to meet a more striking combination of what we most cherish in the historic past of both the North and the South, than in General Atkins' home on Prospect Terrace at Freeport. Hanging along the walls of the hallway, were the General's commissions in the Union army, framed—some signed by Governor Richard Yates and the later ones by Abraham Lincoln. In the library and in the attic there was a wealth of historic matter concerning old North Carolina, including bound volumes of newspapers dated back just after the Revolutionary War, and many documents signed by prominent southern statesmen.
    On the wall hung a silk flag—borne at the Revolutionary battle of Camden. And the southern hospitality—which the writer of this paper enjoyed a short time ago—rested over the whole home."

159 *In 1891, Dot became engaged*
Freeport Journal, December 29, 1891; Atkins Bible (Eleanor and Smith D.). Cobb, a distant cousin, was the son of Needham Bryan Cobb, a Baptist preacher who served in the Civil War, and Martha Louisa Cobb. His great-great-grandfather, Jesse Cobb, married Elizabeth Herritage, whose sister Sarah was married to Richard Caswell.

160 *In 1896, Susie Atkins wed*
Barile; United States, Census; Atkins Bible (Eleanor H. and Smith D.). Susie's children were Susie born in 1897, Smith on March 21, 1898, Jenness on June 5, 1901, Margaret on December 26, 1906, and David on June 8, 1909. An undated letter from Margaret Rackley Poole Martin to her great-nephew, Robert (Jenness's son), notes, "I'm sorry I just don't know a single thing about your Father's Father. His name was John Loose [*sic*]. . . . It is true that when they were divorced my Grandfather insisted that all three children have their names changed to Atkins." Susie's obituary in *Freeport Journal* noted that Loos "preceded her in death. Later she was married to John Rackley, who died several years ago."

160 *Dot's marriage appears to have been strong*
Atkins Bible (Eleanor H. and Smith D.); Barile.

161 *When General Atkins neared retirement*
Freeport Journal, March 18, 1912. After selling the *Journal*, printing office, and bookbindery to Captain A.V. Richards of Galena in 1875, Atkins operated the

Republican during the intervening years and repurchased the *Journal* in 1883, merging it with the *Republican*.

162 *The general remained a popular speaker*

Atkins, "Chickamauga"; Baumgartner, 200; Winship, 71; *Freeport Journal*, March 18, 1912; Atkins, "Lincoln" and "Freeport Debate." In September 1898, Atkins and John T. Wilder, leader of Wilder's Brigade, were among those incorporating Chickamauga Memorial Association to "preserve and. . . ."

164 *By 1913, General Atkins had been editor*

Freeport Journal, March 28, 1913, and April 2, 1913; Atkins, E.H.S., Unpublished, November 6, 1867; Koenig, 118.

165 *Publisher, historian, and friend*

Carpenter, "General," 85; Atkins, Personal Journal. Atkins cared deeply for his hometown. But in his November 24–25, 1854, diary entry, he expressed mixed emotions, noting, "This town of Freeport is lovely to me, if I feel in the least downhearted, for as long as I've lived here, I've not formed an intimate acquaintance. There seems to be a kind of offishness here about everyone that forbids the least approach; a kind of codfish aristocracy that turns up its nose at the stranger who comes not with a recommend in the shape of a broadcloth clothes of the latest style and sporting a cigar case and kid gloves; so I keep a Journal for my companion, and the truth is, it is almost all the companion I have. . . . was I wealthy, friends would flock around me, and I would be invited to their parties and social gatherings, which would add much pleasantry as time wore away. But I am poor."

166 *General Atkins wanted a simple*

Freeport Journal, April 2, 1913; Atkins Bible (Eleanor H. and Smith D.); Swain, "Last Will." (In her will, Mrs. Swain left the Brussels carpet "to Dot & Susa.")

167 *His headstone was made from*

Barile.

167 *That he was buried in Freeport*

Atkins, E.H.S., Unpublished, "My Desolate Home."

Photo Credits

PAGE 29
Mrs. Swain was in her early forties when this portrait was created by an unknown painter. The puffed sleeve and lace collar were popular fashion features in the 1830s and 40s. (Barile Collection)

PAGE 103
This is a reproduction of Ella's letter to her parents following David's death in June 1868. (Barile Collection)

PAGE 125
This photo of Richard (Bunkey) Swain is made from a daguerreotype taken in the late-1860s when high standing collars with wide neckties and stovepipe hats were popular. Also common in that era's portraiture were such mannerisms as the hand tucked in the jacket. (Barile Collection)

PAGE 133
In the early 1880s, Ella wears the gold locket and cameo earrings her husband had given her. The lace jabot was characteristic of the period. The earrings were later made into pins—one for each of her daughters, Dot and Susie. (Barile Collection)

PAGE 143
In December 1881, six months after their mother's death, Dyke, Susie, and Dot pose with their father (perhaps in the parlor of White Hall). All, with the exception of four-year-old Susie, wear mourning clothes. (Barile Collection)

PAGE 157
General Atkins (circa 1890) maintained a busy professional and community schedule for most of his life. (Barile Collection)

PAGE 161
General Atkins (circa 1897) is flanked on the left by Dot and her first child, Smith, and on the right by Susie and her first child, Susie. Dot wears the pin created from one of her mother's cameo earrings. (Barile Collection)

Family Tree

SWAINS

George Edward Swain (June 17, 1763–Dec. 24, 1829) married Caroline Lane Lowry (May 26, 1761–Dec. 25, 1842), widow of David Lowry, in 1789. Their children were:

> Mary, 1781–1819 (father: David Lowry).
>
> James M., 1783–1857 (father: David Lowry).
>
> Charles, 1784–? (father: David Lowry).
>
> Patience, 1787–1851 (father: David Lowry).
>
> Cynthia, 1791–1829.
>
> George Jr., 1792–1877.
>
> Caroline, 1795–1828.
>
> Matilda, 1797–1858.
>
> Althea, 1798–1846.
>
> David, 1801–Aug. 27, 1868; married Eleanor Hope White.
>
> Mary (Polly), 1803–29.

The son of Samuel Swain and Freelove George from England, George Swain was originally from Roxbury, Massachusetts, and moved to Wilkes County, Georgia, where he was a Georgia state legislator and a member of the Georgia Constitutional Convention. He then moved to Asheville. He is buried in the Newton Academy Cemetery.

Caroline Swain was the daughter of Continental Army soldier Jesse Lane, who fought at Valley Forge with General George Washington, and Winnifred Aycock. Her grandfather, Joseph Lane Jr., was born in 1710 in Jamestown, Virginia, where her great-grandfather, Joseph Sr., also was born. Her maternal grandmother, Rebecca Pace Aycock, was born in 1706 in Jamestown, and her maternal grandfather, William Aycock, may have been born there in 1709. She is buried in Big Sandy Mush Methodist Church Cemetery, Leicester.

WHITES

William White (Nov. 2, 1762–Nov. 8, 1811) married Anna Caswell Fonville (Dec. 4, 1766–Feb. 22, 1850) on Aug. 14, 1787. Their children were:

Sarah Richard Caswell, July 9, 1783–? (she was Anna's niece, daughter of her brother Richard Caswell Jr.).

Ann (called Nancy), 1791–Oct. 18, 1860; married Daniel L. Barringer.

Haywood, 1793–1800.

Susannah, Aug. 16, 1795–Oct. 18, 1882.

Elizabeth, Aug. 6, 1797–July 5, 1883; married Boon Felton.

Eleanor Hope, 1800–Feb. 5, 1883; married David L. Swain.

Emma Caswell, Feb. 12, 1802–Sept. 23, 1882.

Gartha, April 5, 1804–July 8, 1824.

Sophronia William, May 23, 1806–Dec. 10, 1876; married John Walker.

Anna Caswell White was the daughter of North Carolina Governor Richard Caswell (son of English immigrant Richard and Christian Dallam Caswell of Joppa, Maryland) and Sarah Herritage (daughter of a well-known planter in New Bern, North Carolina). In 1873 she first married John Fonville who died shortly thereafter.

William, the son of Robert White (Jan. 13, 1736–Jan. 13, 1803) and Eleanor Hope (April 1736–Jan. 14, 1803), was a captain in the N.C. Militia during the Revolutionary War.

ATKINSES

Adna Atkins (Jan. 1, 1789–Aug. 6, 1869) married Sarah Dykins (Dec. 19, 1793–Dec. 18, 1869) on Feb. 19, 1815, in Elmira, NY. Their children were:

Cynthia, 1815–89; married Martin Krinbill; three children, Sarah, Carrie, and Martin.

Mary G., 1817–46; married Austen Bell; daughter, Carrie.

George G., 1820–70s; married Betsy A.; son, Edwin.

Margaret Dykins, 1822–48; married William Hawley; son, William.

John Cherry, 1825–70s; married Harriet; son, John.

Rachel, Sept. 11, 1827–Oct.11, 1827.

Unnamed infant, died in 1828.

Caroline, 1829–55; married Hiram Bright; two daughters, Justine and Caroline.

Hezekiah, 1831–60; married Katie; son, Smith Dykins Atkins.

Smith Dykins, June 9, 1835–March 27, 1913; married Ella Swain.

Louis Eugene, 1839–82; married Elizabeth; son, George.

Adna Atkins was born in 1789 in New Haven, Connecticut. He and Sarah, who was born in 1793 in New Jersey, moved to Freeport, Illinois, in 1848. On Nov. 21, 1854, he purchased about eighty acres in Stephenson County for $600.

Bibliography & References

1789 U.S. Book of Common Prayer, www.justus.anglican.org (accessed May 6, 2009).

"Abraham Lincoln Chronology," lincoln.lib.niu.edu/chronology/abraham_lincoln_chronology.html (accessed June 8, 2009).

"April 1861–Proclamations by President Lincoln and Governor Yates." In "Illinois in the Civil War," www.illinoiscivilwar.org/proclamation1.html (accessed May 6, 2009).

Arthur, John Preston. *Western N.C.: A History. 1730–1919.* Johnson City: Overmountain Press, 1996.

Asheville Daily Citizen. Selected issues.

Atkins Bible (Eleanor H. and Smith D.). Barile Collection. Comprehensive Bible. Philadelphia: Lippincott, 1865.

Atkins Bible (Smith D.). Holy Bible. N.p.

Atkins, E.H.S. Autograph Book.

———. Unpublished letters (1865–68). Barile Collection.

Atkins, Smith D. "Chickamauga: Useless, Disastrous Battle," *Freeport Journal,* 1907.

———. "Decoration Day Address: May 30, 1877," *Freeport Budget,* 1877.

———. "Democracy and *Dred Scott.*" (Address, Freeport: Order of the Joint Executive Committee of the Freeport Wide Awakes, and the Republican Club, 1860.)

———. "Freeport Debate." *Abraham Lincoln: The Tribute of a Century 1809–1909,* ed. Nathan William MacChesney. Chicago: McClurg, 1910.

———. "Historical Sketch of Stephenson County, Ill.," *Freeport Journal,* July 5, 1876.

———. "Lincoln-Douglas Debate." (Address. 1908.)

———. Personal Journal. 1854–55.

———. Personal notes, n.d.

———. Speech, N.Y. State Press Association, June 16, 1885.

———. "Wilder's Brigade," *Freeport Journal*, 1909.

———. "With Sherman's Cavalry." In *Military Essays and Recollections*, ed. Military Order of the Loyal Legion of the United States. Chicago: McClurg, 1894.

Barile, Suzy. Personal Collection.

Barrett, John G. *Sherman's March Through the Carolinas*. Chapel Hill: University of North Carolina Press, 1956.

Battle, Kemp Plummer. *History of the University of North Carolina*. Spartanburg: Reprint Co., 1974.

———. *Memories of an Old-Time Tar Heel*, ed. William James Battle. Chapel Hill: University of North Carolina Press, 1945.

———. "Wilson Caldwell," *North Carolina University Magazine*, v. 14 (1894–95): 315–18.

Baumgartner, Richard A. *Blue Lightning: Wilder's Mounted Infantry Brigade in the Battle of Chickamauga*. Huntington: Blue Acorn, 1997.

Bradley, Mark L. *This Astounding Close*. Chapel Hill: University of North Carolina Press, 2000.

Brecher, Edward M., and editors of *Consumer Reports*. *The Consumers Union Report on Licit and Illicit Drugs*. Special issue. Schaffer Library of Drug Policy, 1972.

Brewer, Fisk P. *Memoir of Hon. David Lowry Swain, LL.D.* Boston: Clapp, 1870.

Britton, Wiley. "A Day With Colonel W.F. Cloud," *Chronicles of Oklahoma* (September 1927): 311+.

Brown, David E. "The Main Attraction," *Carolina Alumni Review* (November/ December 1998): 16–17.

Bulletin, The (Freeport, IL). Selected issues.

Burns, Robert. *Burns*. J.T., ed. London, England: Barnard & Farley, 1819.

Bye, Arthur E. "Portraits Introduce Restorer to University," *Carolina Alumni Review* (December 1943): 95–98.

Caldwell, Bettie D., ed. *Founders and Builders of Greensboro, 1808–1908*. Greensboro: Stone, 1925.

Camp, Cordelia. *David Lowry Swain: Governor and University President.* Asheville: Stephens, 1963.

Carlile, Olga. "Brewster Boast—'Lincoln Slept Here,'" *Journal-Standard*, n.d.

———. "Newspapers in Freeport Have Ups and Downs," *Journal-Standard*, n.d.

Carpenter, Richard V. "General Smith D. Atkins. In Memoriam." Meeting of Illinois State Historical Society, Springfield, IL. May 15–16, 1913.

Carroll, Laurette, "American Quilts of the 19ᵗʰ Century," www.fabrics.net/Laurette19thCentury.asp (accessed May 7, 2009).

Caruthers, E.W. *Interesting Revolutionary Incidents and Sketches of Character Chiefly in the "Old North State."* Philadelphia: Hayes, 1856.

Catalogue of the Trustees, Faculty and Students of the Medical College of the State of South Carolina. Session 1860–61. Charleston: Steam-Powell, 1861.

Chamberlain, Hope Summerell. *Old Days in Chapel Hill.* Chapel Hill: University of North Carolina Press, 1926.

Chapel of the Cross Episcopal Church. Record Book. Chapel Hill, North Carolina.

City Directory. 1894, 1896, 1900, 1912, 1915. Asheville, North Carolina. Richmond: R.L. Polk.

Cobb Loan. Epistolary Correspondence of David Lowry Swain, North Carolina Collection, Wilson Library, University of North Carolina at Chapel Hill.

Committee of Ninety-Second Volunteers. *The Ninety-Second Illinois Volunteers.* Freeport, IL: Journal Steam, 1875.

"A Composite of Years of History," *Journal-Standard*, September 14–15, 1985.

"Confederate Army," Encyclopedia.com, from the *Oxford Companion to American Military History.* John Whiteclay Chambers II, ed. Oxford University Press, 2000. www.encyclopedia.com/doc/1O126-ConfederateArmy.html (accessed June 8, 2009).

Corbett, Anne, and Dallas Smith, "Silent Sentinels of Stone: Old Chapel Hill Cemetery," University of North Carolina at Chapel Hill, www.ibiblio.org/cemetery (accessed May 7, 2009).

Cox, Jacob D. *The March to the Sea: Franklin and Nashville.* New York: Scribner's, 1882.

Culpepper, M.M. *Trials and Triumphs: Women of the American Civil War.* East Lansing: Michigan State University Press, 1992.

Daniels, Josephus. "University Centennial: Sons of the University Celebrating its Birth," *Raleigh State Chronicle*, June 7, 1889.

"David Lowry Swain, 4 Jan. 1801–29 Aug. 1868." *Dictionary of North Carolina Biography*, ed. William S. Powell. Chapel Hill: University of North Carolina Press, 1979.

Davis, George W. *War of the Rebellion: A Compilation of the Official Records of the Union and Confederate Armies*. Washington: GPO, 1894.

"Dear Sis—April 13, 1865." Ypsilanti Historical Museum. Ypsilanti, MI.

Digges, George A., comp. *Buncombe County, North Carolina grantee deed index*. Asheville: Miller Press, 1927.

——. Comp., *Buncombe County, North Carolina grantor deed index*. Asheville: Miller Press, 1926.

Dollar, Ernest A., Jr., "The Battle of Morrisville" (1993), www.mindspring.com/~nixnox/history2.html (accessed May 7, 2009).

Downs, Murray Scott, "Historical Sketch of North Carolina State University," NCSU Faculty Handbook, 1995, www.lib.ncsu.edu/universityarchives/ universityhistory/fac_hand_history.html (accessed June 8, 2009).

Edmunds, Mary Lewis Rucker. *Letters From Edgeworth or The Southernization of Minna Alcott*. Greensboro: Greensboro Preservation Society, 1988.

"Engagement Chronology," Bentonville Battlefield, North Carolina Historic Sites, www.nchistoricsites.org/bentonvi/chronol.htm (accessed June 8, 2009).

Faust, Drew Gilpin. "Altars of Sacrifice: Confederate Women and the Narrative of War," in *Divided Houses: Gender and the Civil War*, ed. Catherine Clinton and Nina Silber. New York: Oxford University Press, 1992.

——. *Mothers of Invention: Women of the Slaveholding South in the American Civil War*. Chapel Hill: University of North Carolina Press, 1996.

Fernow, Berthold. *NY in the Revolution: The Militia—Ulster Co., 3rd Reg.* Cottonport: Polyanthos, 1972.

Finkelman, Paul. *Slavery and the Founders*. Armonk: M.E. Sharpe, 2001.

"The Fire," *The University Magazine*, January 1887: 208–09.

"Former Resident Dies in Tennessee," *Sunday Citizen* (Asheville), July 9, 1911.

Freedmen's Bureau Online, "The Bureau of Refugees, Freedmen, and Abandoned Lands . . ." www.freedmensbureau.com (accessed May 7, 2009).

"Freeport." *World Book Encyclopedia*. Chicago: Field, 1969.

Freeport Journal. Selected issues.

Fulwider, Addison L. *History of Stephenson County Illinois 1880.* Chicago: Clarke, 1910.

"Funeral Services . . ." *Asheville Daily Citizen,* August 5, 1895.

"General Atkins Beloit Address." Reprinted from *Beloit Free Press* (WI), n.d.

Goldsmith, Oliver. *The Deserted Vill*age. Boston: J.E. Tilton, 1866.

Gordon, M., ed. *The American Family in Social-Historical Perspectives.* New York: St. Martin's, 1978.

Graham, John W. Letter to David L. Swain, June 11, 1866, in Walter Clark Papers. North Carolina Office of Archives & History, North Carolina Department of Cultural Resources.

Graham, William Alexander. *The Papers of William Alexander Graham,* Vol. 5–8, ed. Max R. Williams. Raleigh: North Carolina Department of Cultural Resources, 1984.

Green, Virginia Splawn. *The Clayton Clique: The Descendants of George Clayton, 1723–1786.* Part 1. Tampa: V.S. Green, 1995.

Guernsey, Alfred H., and Henry M. Alden. *Harper's Pictorial History of the Civil War.* New York: Fairfax Press, 1866.

Gustason, Harriett. "A Tale of Two Letters: Mystery Man Identified," *Journal-Standard,* February, 22, 2009, www.journalstandard.com/archive/x598681397/A-tale-of-two-letters-mystery-man-identified (accessed June 8, 2009).

Hague, Parthenia Antoinette. *A Blockaded Family: Life in Southern Alabama During the Civil War.* Boston: Houghton, 1888.

Hamilton, J.G. deR. *History of North Carolina,* Vol. 3. Spartanburg: Reprint Co., 1973.

Henderson, Archibald. *The Campus of the First State University.* Chapel Hill: University of North Carolina Press, 1949.

"Historic Oakwood Cemetery." Raleigh: Oakwood Cemetery Business Office, n.d.

Historic Riverside Cemetery. Records. Asheville Parks and Recreation Department. Asheville: City of Asheville, 2008.

"History of the 39th: North Carolina Troops: 1861–1865 39th Regiment N.C.," www.rootsweb.ancestry.com/~nccherok/39threg.html (accessed May 7, 2009).

Holmes, Urban T., Jr. "At the Crossroads on the Hill." Chapel Hill: Chapel of the Cross, 1942.

Hurlbut, Stephen A., "Reports of Brig. Gen. Stephen A. Hurlbut, U.S. Army, Commanding Fourth Division, Army of Tennessee. April 6–7, 1862," Series 1—Volume X/1 [S#10], www.civilwarhome.com/hurlbutshilohor. htm (accessed May 7, 2009).

In the Footprints of the Pioneers of Stephenson County, Ill.: A Genealogical Record. Freeport: Pioneer, 1900.

"In the Haven of Rest," *Asheville Daily Citizen,* August 2, 1895.

Isaac, Peggy. Personal Collection.

Ivey, Pete. "Town & Gown," *Chapel Hill News,* December 15, 1963.

Jones, H.G. *For History's Sake.* Chapel Hill: University of North Carolina Press, 1966.

——. *North Carolina Illustrated.* Chapel Hill: University of North Carolina Press, 1983.

Jones, J.B. *A Rebel War Clerk's Diary at the Confederate States Capital.* Philadelphia: Lippincott, 1866.

Jones, Joseph. Medical Officers of Army of Tennessee. Joseph Jones Papers. Special Collections, Hill Memorial Library, Louisiana State University Libraries, Baton Rouge. (Revised 2000.)

Jones, Joseph Seawell. "Historical Society," *Raleigh Register,* November 18, 1834.

Journal and Republican (Freeport, IL). Selected issues.

Journal of the House of Representatives of the General Assembly of the State of North Carolina at its Session 1909. Raleigh: E.M. Uzzell, 1909.

Journal of the Senate of the General Assembly of the State of North Carolina at its Session 1909. Raleigh: E.M. Uzzell, 1909.

Journal Standard (Freeport, IL). Selected issues.

Koenig, Robert F., comp. *Camera Studies of Freeport, Illinois.* Freeport: Wagner, 1954.

Lea, Benjamin J. "Reports of Cases Argued and Determined in the Supreme Court of Tennessee for the Eastern Division, September Term, 1881 . . . for the Middle Division, December Term, 1881 . . . for the Western Division, April Term, 1882," Vol. 8. Nashville: Tavel, Law Book Publisher, 1882.

Lefler, H.W., and P. Stanford, eds. *North Carolina.* 2nd edition. New York: Harcourt, 1972.

Leloudis, James L. "Civil War and Reconstruction," "Documenting the American South," UNC University Library, www.docsouth.unc.edu (accessed May 31, 2009).

Leonard, Elizabeth D. *Yankee Women: Gender Battles in the Civil War.* New York: Norton, 1995.

London, Lawrence Foushee, and Sarah McCulloh Lemmon, eds. *Episcopal Church in North Carolina, 1701–1959.* Raleigh: Episcopal Diocese of NC, 1987.

Lyman, Theodore. *Meade's Headquarters, 1863–1865,* ed. George E. Agassiz. Boston: Atlantic Monthly, 1922.

Madden, David, ed. *Beyond the Battlefield: The Ordinary Life and Extraordinary Times of the Civil War Soldier.* New York: Touchstone, 2000.

Mallett, Charles P. Excerpts from Letter of Charles P. Mallett to Charles B. Mallett, 18 Apr. 1865. "Documenting the American South," UNC University Library, www.docsouth.unc.edu (accessed May 8, 2009).

"Marriages," *Weekly Record* (Raleigh), September 2, 1865.

"Married," *North-West Newspaper* (Freeport, IL), September 13–14, 1865.

Maynard, Eleanor Hope Newell. Letter to James Reston. September 16, 1995. Barile Collection.

McGuire, Judith. *Diary of a Southern Refugee, During the War.* Richmond: J.W. Randolph, 1889.

Meeting of the Executive Committee. March 7, 1908. *Inventory of the Board of Trustees of the University of North Carolina Records, 1789–1932.* Vol. S-11. Collection No. 40001. University Archives, Wilson Library, University of North Carolina at Chapel Hill.

Mintz, Steven, *"Digital History,"* www.digitalhistory.uh.edu (accessed May 8, 2009).

Moore, Mary Gudger. "Some Early Recollections of Asheville and Western North Carolina." Written at request of John P. Arthur. Special Collections, D. Hiden Ramsey Library, University of North Carolina, Asheville.

Morphis, B. "The Southern Belle and the Union General," *News and Observer* (Raleigh), January 31, 1965: 2.

"Mrs. Clayton Struck by Car, Taken by Death," *Asheville Times,* September 24, 1947.

Murray, Elizabeth Reid. *Wake: Capital County of North Carolina,* Vol. 1. Raleigh: Capital, 1983.

National Governors Association. "North Carolina Governor David Lowry Swain," www.nga.org (accessed May 8, 2009).

"N.C. Revolutionary War Records of Primary Interest to Genealogists," North Carolina Office of Archives & History, North Carolina Department of Cultural Resources, www.archives.ncdcr.gov/FindingAids/Circulars/AIC13.pdf (accessed June 8, 2009).

Newell, Wuff. "Ellie Swain's Marriage to Gen. Atkins is Story of Deepest Love and Devotion," *Greensboro Daily News*, August 28, 1949.

New Testament of Our Lord and Savior Jesus Christ. New York: American Bible Society, 1857.

North Carolina Standard (Raleigh), April 30, 1862.

"Nursery of Patriotism: The University at War, 1861–1945," Exhibit, Wilson Library, University of North Carolina at Chapel Hill, www.lib.unc.edu/mss/exhibits (accessed May 8, 2009).

Oberholtzer, Ellis Paxson. *A History of the United States Since the Civil War*. New York: Macmillan, 1917.

"Old Chapel Hill Cemetery," National Register of Historic Places Registration Form, U.S. Department of the Interior, National Park Service. October 1990, townhall.townofchapelhill.org/facilities/cemeteries/old_cemetery/history/national_register/ (accessed May 31, 2009).

O'Malley, Leslie C. "The Perils of Pauline: Challenges Facing Mid-19th Century Ontario County Women," raims.com/THEPERILSOFPAULINE.html (accessed May 8, 2009).

Orange County, North Carolina, Marriage Bonds.

"Overview of the Civil War in Kentucky," Kentucky and the Civil War, KET EdWeb Site, www.ket.org/civilwar/kyrole.html (accessed June 8, 2009).

Parish Register 1890–1900. Trinity Parish, Asheville, NC.

Perry, Benjamin F. *Reminiscences of Public Men*. Philadelphia: Avil, 1883.

Perry, Leslie J., ed. *The War of the Rebellion*. U.S. War Records Office. U.S. War Dept. Washington: GPO, 1895.

Peters, Peter, "History of the Battle of Aiken," Brigadier General Bernard E. Bee Camp # 1575, www.battleofaiken.org (accessed June 8, 2009).

Phillips, Charles. Untitled. *North Carolina Presbyterian* (Fayetteville), September 23, 1868.

Phillips, Gordon. *Best Foot Forward: Chas. A. Blatchford & Sons Ltd. (Artificial Limb Specialists), 1890–1990*. Cambridge, Eng.: Granta, 1990.

Platter, Cornelius C., "Cornelius C. Platter Civil War Diary, 1864–1865," Digital Library of Georgia, dlg.galileo.usg.edu/hargrett/platter/ (accessed May 8, 2009).

Portrait and Biographical Album of Stephenson County, Ill. Chicago: Chapman, 1888.

Powell, William S. *The First State University.* Chapel Hill: University of North Carolina Press, 1972.

———. *North Carolina: A Bicentennial History.* New York: Norton, 1977.

"Preserving Chapel Hill's Past for Future Generations," Chapel Hill Historical Society, www.ibiblio.org/chhistsoc (accessed May 31, 2009).

Psalms and Hymns. Philadelphia: Presbyterian, 1843.

Public Laws of the State of North Carolina, Passed by the General Assembly, at its Session of 1868–1869. Raleigh: State Printer and Bindery, 1869.

Public Laws & Resolutions of the State of North Carolina, Passed by the General Assembly, at its Session of 1909. Raleigh: E.M. Uzzell, 1909.

Rable, G.C. *Civil Wars: Women and the Crisis of Southern Nationalism.* Urbana: University of Illinois Press, 1989.

Raleigh Sentinel. Selected issues.

Register of Deeds. Buncombe County. Asheville, NC.

Rubin, Karen Aviva. *Aftermath of Sorrow: White Women's Search for Their Lost Cause, 1861–1917.* Tallahassee: Florida State University, 2007.

Russell, Phillips. *The Woman Who Rang the Bell.* Chapel Hill: University of North Carolina Press, 1949.

Scott, Anne Firor, General Introduction, "Southern Women and Their Families in the 19th Century," Southern Historical Collection, Wilson Library, University of North Carolina at Chapel Hill, srnels.people.wm.edu/sources/swmna8.htm (accessed June 8, 2009).

"Second Summer," Abraham Jacobi. *Encyclopaedic Index of Medicine and Surgery,* ed. Edward J. Bermingham. New York: Bermingham, 1882.

Silber, Nina. "A Woman's War: Gender and Civil War Studies," *OAH Magazine of History* (Fall 1993): 11–13.

———. "The Northern Myth of the Rebel Girl" in *Women of the American South,* ed. Christie Anne Farnham. New York: New York University Press, 1997.

Smith, Charles Lee. *The History of Education in North Carolina.* Washington: GPO, 1888.

Snider, William D. *Light on the Hill.* Chapel Hill: University of North Carolina Press, 1992.

Southeastern Reporter, Vol. 64. St. Paul: West Publishing, 1909.

Spahn, Joyce. "A Community Recovers a Treasure: The Freeport District Carousel," *Illinois Parks & Recreation* 26.6, 1995.

Spencer, Cornelia P. Spencer Papers. North Carolina Office of Archives & History, North Carolina Department of Cultural Resources.

———. *First Steps in North Carolina History.* Raleigh: Williams, 1890.

———. Letter from Eleanor Swain Atkins to Cornelia Phillips Spencer. "Documenting the American South," UNC University Library, www.docsouth.unc.edu (accessed May 8, 2009).

———. *The Last Ninety Days of the War in North Carolina.* New York: Watchman, 1866.

———. "The Late Hon. D.L. Swain," *Raleigh Sentinel*, August 29, 1868.

———. "Proceedings of the Grand Lodge of North Carolina."

———. Untitled. *North Carolina Presbyterian* (Fayetteville), August 27, 1868.

Sterkx, H.E. *Partners in Rebellion: Alabama Women in the Civil War.* Rutherford: Fairleigh Dickinson University Press, 1970.

Stolpen, S. *Chapel Hill: A Pictorial History.* Norfolk: Donning, 1978.

Stoops, Martha. *The Heritage: The Education of Women at St. Mary's College, Raleigh, North Carolina, 1842–1982.* Raleigh: St. Mary's, 1984.

Swain Bible. Barile Collection. The Holy Bible. Cooperstown: H. & E. Phinney, 1844.

Swain, David L. Manuscripts Division, North Carolina Office of Archives & History, North Carolina Department of Cultural Resources.

———. Address delivered at opening of Tucker Hall. August 24, 1867.

Swain, E.W. Unpublished letters. Barile Collection.

———. "Last Will of . . ."

"Swain, Richard C." "Documenting the American South," UNC University Library, www.docsouth.unc.edu (accessed May 8, 2009).

Tepper, Steven J. *Chronicles of the Bicentennial Observance of the University of North Carolina.* Chapel Hill: University of North Carolina (1998): 134–35.

"To Name U.S. Armory Here," *Journal-Standard* (Freeport, IL), n.d.

UNC Bicentennial. Chapel Hill: University of North Carolina, 1993.

UNC General Alumni Assn. *2002 Alumni Directory,* Chapel Hill: University of North Carolina, 2002.

United States. Census Records, www.ancestry.com (accessed May 8, 2009).

Vance, Zebulon Baird. *The Life and Character of Hon. David L. Swain.* Durham: Blackwell, 1878.

———. *Papers of Zebulon Baird Vance,* Vol. 1, ed. Frontis W. Johnston. Raleigh: North Carolina Department of Archives and History, 1963.

Vickers, J., et al. *Chapel Hill: An Illustrated History.* Chapel Hill: Barclay, 1985.

———. *Images of America: Chapel Hill.* Charleston: Arcadia, 1966.

Wagner, Frederick B. Jr., MD, ed. *Thomas Jefferson University—Tradition and Heritage.* 1989. jdc.jefferson.edu/wagner2.

Wagstaff, Henry McGilbert. *Impressions of Men and Movements at the University of North Carolina.* Chapel Hill: University of North Carolina Press, 1950.

Walbert, Kathryn. Excerpt of Oral History with Edwin Caldwell Jr. of Chapel Hill. Southern Oral History Program, Interview No. L-091, July 6,1995.

"The War for Southern Independence: The Civil War in North Carolina," www.researchonline.net/nccw/mastindx.htm (accessed June 8, 2009).

Waugh, Elizabeth Culbertson, et al. *North Carolina's Capital, Raleigh.* Chapel Hill: University of North Carolina Press, 1972.

Wells, Reba. "In Their Own Words: Diaries of 19th Century Women." Lecture.

White, William. "Last Will and Testament." Barile Collection.

Wiley, Bell Irvin. *Confederate Women.* Westport: Greenwood, 1975.

Williams, Charles Richard, ed. *Diary and Letters of Rutherford B. Hayes.* Columbus: Ohio State Archeological and Historical Society, 1922.

Williams, S.D., ed. "The University of North Carolina at Chapel Hill: A Historical Tour," *UNC Bicentennial.* Chapel Hill: University of North Carolina, 1993.

Wills, Charles W. *Army Life of an Illinois Soldier.* Washington, DC: Globe Printing, 1906.

Wilson, Louis R., ed. *Historical Sketches.* Durham: Moore, 1976.

———. *Selected Papers of Cornelia Phillips Spencer.* Chapel Hill: University of North Carolina Press, 1953.

Winship, Amy Davis. *My Life Story.* Boston: Richard G. Badger, 1920.

Wise, Jim. *On Sherman's Trail: The Civil War's North Carolina Climax.* Charleston: History Press, 2008.

Woodfin, Nicholas W. Papers #1689, Southern Historical Collection, Wilson Library, University of North Carolina at Chapel Hill.

Index

Adams, John Quincy, 36

American Revolutionary War, 11, 13, 33, 34, 142, 181n, 189n, 195n, 202n, 207, 208

Army of the Cumberland, 156–58, 162

Army of the Tennessee, 53–54, 156–58, 180–81n

Asheville, North Carolina, 37, 40–41, 94, 181n, 187n, 194–96n, 201n, 207

Astor, John Jacob III, 75–76

Atkins, Adna Stanly, 11, 51, 92–93, 122, 179–80n, 193n, 209. *See also* Atkins, Sarah

Atkins, David H., 11

Atkins, David Swain, 89–91, 101–05, 116–17, 124, 128, 165, 198n. *See also* Atkins, Eleanor (Ella); Second summer disease

Atkins, Eleanor Hope (Dot), 122, 123, 132, 136, 137, 141, 143, 152, 156, 159–60, 161, 164, 200–01n, 202n, 203n, 205. *See also* Atkins, Eleanor (Ella); Atkins, Smith D.

Atkins, Eleanor (Ella) Hope Swain: Atkins, Smith D., introduction to, 13–16, 173n; birth, 82; childhood, 4–5, 41–43, 137, 184n, 204; courtship & betrothal, 19–22, 25, 28, 29–30, 43–46, 61, 62, 159, 173–74n, 175n, 176n, 178–79n, 182n, 183n; death of, 134–38, 167; education, 42–43, 177n, 178n; Freeport, 71–72; grandparents, 184n, 207, 208; housekeeping, 89, 90–93, 96–97, 120, 164; letters, xiii, 71–73, 89–92, 95–105, 115–20, 127, 136, 138, 148, 167, 185n; marriage, xiii, 71–73, 75, 77–78, 89, 90, 92, 96–98, 101, 104–05, 110, 115–17, 119–20, 124, 128, 131, 134–36, 138, 146–50, 158–59, 165, 167, 209; photographs, 5, 24, 133; pregnancies and childbirths, 73, 75, 77, 89, 120, 122, 123, 126, 128–29, 132, 185n, 194n; religion, 43, 102–04, 115, 117, 124, 178n; slaves, 90–91; Swain, Richard (Bunkey), 4–5, 93–95, 105, 116, 124, 136, 148, 189n; wedding, 61–66, 166, 182n; wedding ring, xiii, 65, 182–83n. *See also* Swain, Anne; Swain, David; Swain, Eleanor White; Swain, Richard Caswell; *and individual names of children*

Atkins, Louis, 201n, 209

Atkins, Richard Swain, 128, 156

Atkins, Sarah Dykins, 51, 92–93, 122–23, 193n, 209

Atkins, Smith Dykins (Gen.): Atkins, Dyke, death of, 155–56; Atkins, Eleanor (Ella),
     death of, 134–38; Atkins, Eleanor (Ella), introduction to, 13–16; childhood, 11,
     51–52, 127, 172n, 196n; death of, 164–67, 209; education, 11, 51–52; enlistment, 11–12,
     52–53, 167, 180n; Freeport, 11, 49–50, 90, 116, 120, 127–28, 156–58, 162–65, 179n, 197n,
     202n, 203n, 205; Graham, William, 47, 63, 185n; grandchildren, 159–61, 165, 202n;
     Johnson, Andrew, 73–74, 97, 98, 179n, 189–90n; Kilpatrick, Judson, 10–11, 46, 167;
     legal career, 11, 52, 74, 104, 123; Lincoln, Abraham, 11, 50, 52, 59, 163, 202n; married
     life, 71–73, 75–78, 89, 92, 96–98, 101, 104–05, 110, 115–17, 119–20, 123–24, 128, 131,
     134–38, 146, 148–50, 156–59, 165–67; military career, 11–12, 24, 28–30, 49–50, 53–59,
     62, 156, 158, 162, 180–81n; military discharge, 28–30, 59; newspaper career, 51–52,
     123, 128, 155–56, 161–64, 166–67, 202n; Ninety–second Illinois Volunteers, 10, 19–20,
     26, 28–30, 49, 54, 56, 90, 123, 128, 159; parents, 51–52, 92–93, 122–23; photographs,
     26, 143, 157, 161; poetry, 20–22, 77, 174–75n; political life, 11, 52, 74, 98, 116, 146–47,
     156, 164, 189–90n, 201–02n; postmaster, 59, 62, 73, 90, 97–98, 104, 189–90n; reli-
     gion, 75, 124, 164; Republican Party, 73, 146, 164; rumors of stealing, 46–47, 63–64,
     178–79n; slavery, 12, 54–56; Stephenson County Soldiers' Monument, 90, 121, 187n;
     Swain, David, 11–16, 33–34, 67–68, 176n, 178–79n; Swain, Eleanor White, 25, 141,
     148–50, 155, 199n; war, thoughts on, 12, 27, 28–29, 50, 57, 117, 121, 147, 162, 180n, 181n,
     202n; widower, 158–59, 202n, 203n. See also Atkins, Eleanor (Ella); Chapel Hill,
     Union army occupation; and individual names of children

Atkins, Smith Dykins (Dyke), 126, 132, 136, 141, 152–53, 155–56, 205; photograph, 143

Atkins, Susan Annie, 132, 136, 141, 156, 160–61, 198n, 202n, 205; photographs, 143, 161

Atkins, Swain Graham, 75, 124, 128, 167, 185n

Autograph books, 22, 175n

Barnett, John C., 185n

Barringer, Ann (Nancy) White, 94, 189n, 192n, 208

Barringer, Daniel L., 94, 208

Bates, F.J., 164

Battle, Junius, 5

Battle, Kemp P., 2, 5–6, 10, 36, 76–77, 178–79n

Battle, Wesley Lewis, 5

Battle, William H. (Judge), 2, 5, 10, 47, 137, 142, 144–45. See also Battle, Kemp P.

Bentonville, Battle of, 5, 57, 181n

Black Codes, 73, 185n. See also Freedmen's Bureau

Bragg, Braxton (Gen.). See Chickamauga

Breckinridge, J.C. (Gen.), 76

Brewster House, 71–72, 163, 184n

Bright, Hiram, 52, 209

Buchanan, James, 111

Buncombe County, 34–36, 41, 152, 170n, 191n, 194n

Burchard, H.C., 123, 146

Burgess, Rosa, 10, 172n

Burns, Robert, 116–17

Burt, Susan E. *See* Swain, Susan Burt

Caldwell, Wilson Swain. *See* Swain, Wilson

Carpenter, Richard V., 165, 202n

Caswell, Richard, 34, 142, 202n, 208

Chapel Hill: effects of war, 4–7, 12, 23, 25–27, 33–34, 44–46, 63, 170n, 182n; reaction to
    Swain/Atkins betrothal, 33–34, 44–46, 61–68, 76–77, 183n; Reconstruction, 67–68,
    75–77, 106–08, 118–19, 130, 144–45, 150–51, 185n; Union army occupation, 1–4, 10–13,
    19–20, 23–28, 46–47, 169n, 170n, 178–179n, 183n; university life, 1, 3–5, 6, 23–27,
    45–46, 75–77, 98, 106–08, 111–12, 130–31, 169n, 170n, 191n, 197–98n; Wheeler's
    troops, 3–4, 7, 9, 10, 170n. *See also* University of North Carolina

Chapel of the Cross Episcopal Church, 12–13, 64–65, 86, 173n, 175n, 178n, 182n, 186n

Chattanooga, Tennessee. *See* Chickamauga

Chicago Tribune, 52

Chickamauga, Battle of, 56, 162, 203n

Civil War: economic hardships, 6, 7, 26–28, 45–47, 63, 72, 75–77, 106–07, 175n, 189n;
    surrender, 1, 7, 170–72n; women, 3, 4, 6, 7, 13–14, 16, 19, 23, 25, 28, 29, 34, 41, 47, 53,
    63, 72, 148–50, 177n. *See also* Chapel Hill, effects of war; Chapel Hill, Union
    army occupation; Confederacy; Kilpatrick, Judson; Raleigh, surrender; Sherman,
    William T.; *and individual battles*

Clayton, Eleanor Louise (Lula) Swain Grant. *See* Swain, Eleanor Louise

Clinton, Georgia, 57

Cobb, Eleanor Hope Atkins. *See* Atkins, Eleanor Hope (Dot)

Cobb, Needham Tyndale, 159–60, 161, 202n. *See also* Atkins, Eleanor Hope (Dot)

Cockley, D.L. (Capt.), 21–22, 175n, 193n

Coleman, Cynthia Swain, 189n, 207

Coleman, David, 94, 189n

Columbia, South Carolina, 57

Concord, North Carolina, 29, 30

Confederacy, 1, 6–7, 13, 73–74, 146, 162, 169n, 171–72n, 184n. *See also* Spencer,
    Cornelia Phillips

Confederate army, 1–9, 57, 94–95, 171n, 189n

Constitutional Convention of 1865, 75

"Cotter's Saturday Night, The." *See* Burns, Robert

Cox, W.R. (Gen.), 76

Culpepper, Marilyn Meyer, 25, 177n, 184n

Daniels, Josephus, 111
Davis, Jefferson (Pres. of the Confederacy), 76
Davis, John A., 163
"Deserted Village, The." *See* Goldsmith, Oliver
Domestic life, 90–93, 96–97, 177n. *See also* Women, domesticity
Douglas, Stephen (U.S. Sen.), 56, 72, 158, 163. *See also* Lincoln-Douglas Debates
Douglass, Frederick, 56
Dred Scott, 12

Edgecombe County, North Carolina, 152
Edgeworth Female Seminary, 42–43, 177n. *See also* Atkins, Eleanor (Ella), education;
    Greensboro; Morehead, John Motley; Sterling, Richard; women, education
Eleventh Illinois Volunteers (Company A), 58, 180n
Ellis, R.B., 37
Emery, Thomas R., MD, 108
Evening Journal (Chicago), 146, 147

Family tree: Atkins, 209; Swain, 207; White, 208
Felton, Betsy White, 64, 83, 84–85, 118, 187–88n, 192n, 199n, 208
Fetter, Fred, 4
Fetter, Manuel (Prof.), 4, 108
Fetter, Sarah Cox, 66, 83
Fetter, Susan, 23, 25
Fetter, Will, 4
Finch, Edward, 158
Fort Donelson, Tennessee, 53, 180n
Fort Henry, Tennessee, 53, 180n
Fourth Texas Regiment, 6
Freedmen, 65, 73, 184–85n
Freedmen's Bureau, 73, 184–85n. *See also* Black Codes
Freeport: history, 183–84n; honoring soldiers, 12, 49, 90, 121, 187n; life in, 49–52, 58–59,
    71–74, 90, 97–98, 119, 121, 161–62, 166–67; winter weather, 77, 127, 196–97n. *See also*
    Atkins, Smith D.; *Freeport Bulletin; Freeport Journal*; Stephenson County Soldier's
    Monument
Freeport Bulletin, 123, 135, 136
Freeport Journal, 49, 54, 66, 74, 110, 121–24, 126, 128, 146, 155, 161–62, 164, 166, 167, 202n

Gales, Joseph, 34, 188n
Gales, W.R., 34

Gaston, William, 34

Gatlin, Mary, 25, 95, 175n

Gatlin, Richard, 83

Gettysburg, 5

Goldsmith, Oliver, 77–78

Goodrich & Scoville, 52

Governor's Palace, 82, 186n

Grace Episcopal Church. *See* Zion Episcopal Church

Graham, John W., 63, 64, 178–79n

Graham, Susan, 63

Graham, William A. (Gov.): Atkins, Smith D., 47, 63, 184–85n; Civil War, 8–9,
     171–72n; correspondence, David Swain, 8, 11, 12, 33, 41, 47, 49, 71, 75, 81, 85, 89, 106,
     169n, 170–72n, 176n, 177n, 178–79n, 184n, 185n, 186n, 187n, 191n; North Carolina
     Historical Society, 144–45; Raleigh, surrender, 8–9, 171–72n; Reconstruction, 145;
     Swain papers, 144–45

Greensboro, North Carolina, 29, 42–43. *See also* Atkins, Eleanor (Ella), education;
     Edgeworth Female Seminary

Griswoldville, Battle of, 57

Hague, Parthenia A., 63

Hale, E.J., 179n

Hamilton, W.D. (Col.), 14–15

Hawks, Cicero, 83

Haywood, Fabius, MD, 8

Haywood, John, 40

Herbert, B.B., 161–62, 163

Herrick, Jack. *See* Red Clay Ramblers

Herritage, Elizabeth, 202n

Herritage, Sarah, 202n, 208

Hicks, George (Col.), 74

Hillsborough (Hillsboro), 28–29, 47, 178–79n

Holden, W.W., 76

Holmes, Urban T., Jr., 173–74n

Hooper, Mary E., 83

Hooper, William, 43, 145

Hubbard, Fordyce M. *See* Chapel of the Cross

Hubbard, Martha H., 66

Hurlbut, Stephen A. (Brig. Gen.), 53–54, 180–81n

Ice King and the Sweet South Wind, The, 132
Illinois Constitution of 1848, 56
Illinois Republicans, 73, 146
Illinois State Historical Society, 15–16, 163
Illinois Woman's School, 156
In the Footprints of the Pioneers of Stephenson County, Ill., 58, 180n
Interesting Revolutionary Incidents, 33

Johnson, Andrew (U.S. Pres.), 73–74, 97–98, 106, 111, 179n, 189–90n.
    See also Freedmen's Bureau; Reconstruction
Johnston, Joseph E. (Gen.), 2, 28
Johnston, Robert D. (Gen.), 76
Jones, J.B., 6
Jones, Johnston B., MD, 94
Jones, Pride, 47, 178–79n
Jones, Rebecca Edwards, 47, 178–79n
Jordan, Thomas J. (Gen.), 47, 178–79n
Journal. See Freeport Journal
Journal and Republican, 155

Kane County Democrat, 52
Kemper Hall, 156
Kentucky, 54–55. *See also* Mount Sterling; Slavery
Kilpatrick, Judson C. (Gen.), 1, 9, 10–11, 28, 29, 46, 167, 169n.
    See also Chapel Hill, Union army occupation
Krinbill, Cynthia Atkins, 72, 75, 184n, 193n, 201n, 209
Krinbill, Martin, 72, 75, 120, 201n, 209

Lane, Jesse, 207
Lane, Joel, 34, 176n
Lane, Joseph, 176n
Lee, Robert E. (Gen.), 1, 76
Lincoln, Abraham, 11, 50, 52, 54, 57, 59, 158, 163, 176n, 180n, 181n, 202n.
    See also Atkins, Smith D.; Lincoln-Douglas Debates
Lincoln-Douglas Debates, 72, 163, 203n; Fiftieth Anniversary, 158, 163; Society, 158
Lowry, James, 36

Macon, Georgia, 57
Mallett, Charles P., 1, 2, 5, 23, 47

Mallett, Edward, 5

Mallett, Richardson, 5

Mallett, William P., MD, 94

Marriages, North–South, xiii, 14, 33–34, 41–42, 45–47, 66–68, 135, 137, 176n.
    See also Atkins, Eleanor (Ella)

Martin, William J., 4

McGuire, Judith W.B., 63

McPheeters, William (Rev.), 193n

Monroe's Crossroads, North Carolina, 57

Morehead, John Motley (Gov.), 42. *See also* Atkins, Eleanor (Ella), education;
    Edgeworth Female Seminary

Morrisville Station, 3, 169–70n

Mount Sterling, 54–56. *See also* Atkins, Smith D., military career; Slavery

Mt. Morris Gazette, 51

National Printer–Journalist. See Herbert, B.B.

New York State Press Association, 155

Newell, Eleanor ("Wuff") Hope, xiii, 25, 141, 150, 158, 183n

Newspapers. *See individual newspapers*

Ninth Ohio Cavalry, 14

Ninety–second Illinois Volunteers, 3, 10, 19–20, 28–30, 49, 54–56, 166, 170n, 181n;
    Ninety–Second Illinois Volunteers, 27, 128, 159; reunion, 90, 123

North Carolina College of Agriculture and Mechanic Arts, 106–07

North Carolina Historical Society, 142, 144–45, 199n, 200n

North Carolina House of Commons, 36–37, 40–41

North Carolina Presbyterian, 109–10

North Carolina School for the Deaf, 19

North Carolina State University, 106–07

Oakwood Cemetery, 119, 135, 192–93n

Old South (building), 64–65

Opiate use, 84–85

Pawling, Levi (Col.), 11

Pecatonica River, 51, 184n

Perry, Benjamin F., 177n

Phillips, Charles (Prof.), 2, 108–10, 126, 137

Phillips, James, 110

Phillips, Samuel, 64

Polk, James K. (U.S. Pres.), 111
Pool, Solomon, 118–19, 192–93n
Powder Springs, Battle of, 57
Powell, William S., xiii, 46
Prairie Democrat, 51
President's House, 4, 63–65, 81, 86, 99, 108–09, 111, 118–19, 142, 170n
Prospect Terrace, 89–93, 160, 161, 164, 166, 202n

Rackley, Susan Annie Atkins Loos. *See* Atkins, Susan Annie
Raleigh, North Carolina: effects of war, 2, 7; establishment, 34, 176n; surrender of, 3,
     8–10, 45, 171–72n. *See also* Governor's Palace; Oakwood Cemetery; White Hall
Raleigh Register, 34, 135
Raleigh Sentinel, 66, 67
Raleigh State *Chronicle*, 111
Rawlins, John A. (Capt.), 54
Ray, Lavender R., 4, 170n
Reconstruction, 14, 46, 64, 67–68, 73–77, 106–08, 118, 131, 142, 144–45, 183n, 189–90n,
     191n, 192–93n. *See also* Freedmen; Freedmen's Bureau; Johnson, Andrew;
     University of North Carolina
Red Clay Ramblers, 173n
Register, 52
Republican, 202n
Republican Party, 73, 97, 146, 163–64, 173n, 189–90n, 197n, 201n
Richards, A.V. (Capt.), 202n
Rifle. *See* Spencer Repeating Rifle
Rock River Seminary, 51
Ruffin, John S., 37

Saint Mary's School, 43, 141, 178n. *See also* Atkins, Eleanor (Ella); Atkins, Eleanor
     Hope (Dot); Smedes, Aldert; women, education
Salisbury, North Carolina, 29, 75, 188n
Saunders, William L. (Treas.), 151
Savanna, Illinois, 52
Savannah, Georgia, 1–2, 57, 169n
Schermerhorn, J.M. (Capt.), 10
Schoonmaker, Frederick (Capt.), 11
Second Brigade of Kilpatrick's Cavalry, 10, 28–30, 167
Second summer disease, 101–02, 190n
Serenading, 19, 20, 174n
Servants, 12–13, 47, 152, 178–79n, 184n. *See* Slavery

Shannon, Illinois, 93, 96, 116, 124, 152, 189n

Shelbyville, Tennessee, 94, 95, 126, 194–96n

Sherman, William T. (Gen.), 1, 2, 3, 8–9, 10, 16, 27, 45–46, 171n

Sherman's March to the Sea, 57

Shiloh, Battle of, 53–54, 163

Simpson, Bland. *See* Red Clay Ramblers

Slavery, 10, 12–13, 54–56, 86, 90–91, 93, 171n, 173n, 192n; education of, 10, 73, 172n, 184–85n. *See also* Atkins, Smith D.; *Dred Scott*; Freedmen; Freedmen's Bureau; Reconstruction; Swain, David L.; Swain, Eleanor White; Swain, Wilson

Smedes, Aldert (Rev.), 43, 178n

Smith, Charles Lee, 16, 49

Sons of Veterans No. 400 (S.D. Atkins Chapter), 158

Spencer, Cornelia Phillips: Atkins, Eleanor (Ella), 42, 123, 132, 137; Atkins, Smith D., 62, 65, 199n; Chapel Hill, 2–7, 9, 25–26, 46, 131; North Carolina Historical Society, 144–45, 151, 155, 200n; Swain, Anne, 83, 85–86, 94, 190n; Swain, David, 36, 106–08, 110–12, 119, 176n, 197–98n; Swain, Eleanor White, 127, 131, 137, 141, 197–98n; Swain, Richard Caswell, 126, 194–96n; Swain/Atkins courtship & wedding, xiii, 13, 16, 22, 28–30, 33–34, 44–45, 61–65, 67–68, 75–76, 178–79n; Vance, Zebulon, 62, 76, 131

Spencer Repeating Rifle, 181n

State Military Academy of Louisiana. *See* Sherman, William T.

Steele, Bailey Peyton (Dick), 126–27, 194–96n

Steele, Margaret Louisa. *See* Swain, Margaret Louisa

Stephens, Alexander H. (V.P. of Confederacy), 73

Stephenson County, 11, 50, 58, 167, 173n, 180n, 209

Stephenson County Old Settlers, 156

Stephenson County Soldiers' Monument, 50, 90, 121, 187n

Sterling, Richard, 42. *See also* Edgeworth Female Seminary

Summerell, Mrs. J.J., 75, 76

Sumter, South Carolina, 52, 58–59, 173n, 180n

Swain, Anne, 3, 7, 41, 42, 64, 71, 82–83, 129, 178n, 184n; cancer, 81, 85–86; death of, 86, 89, 95, 98, 101, 109, 111, 119, 136, 187n, 190n, 199n; mental illness, 41–42, 81, 82–85; opium use, 84–85; reinterment, 118–19, 192–93n

Swain, Bunkey. *See* Swain, Richard Caswell

Swain, Caroline Lowry, 184n, 187–89n, 207

Swain, David (Infant), 82, 128

Swain, David, Jr., 82, 111, 128, 178n; reinterment, 118–19, 192–93n

Swain, David L.: accident & death of, 108–12, 118, 131, 141, 191n; Anne, death of 85–86, 186n; Atkins, Smith D., 11–16, 33–34, 49, 59, 67–68, 176n, 178–79n; Buncombe County, 34–36, 41, 152, 170n, 191n, 194n; education, 34, 36, 187–88n; Ella, engagement & marriage of, 33–34, 44–46, 49, 59, 61–62, 68, 92, 176n, 183n; governor, North Carolina, 6, 8, 62, 82, 186n; Graham, William, 8–9, 12, 47, 63, 81, 85, 123,

169n, 170–72n, 176n, 177n, 178–79n, 184n, 185n, 186n, 187n, 191n, 192n; Johnson, Andrew, 98, 106, 111–12; legal career, 36–37, 41; North Carolina Historical Society, 142–45, 151, 199n; papers of, 142–145, 151, 199n, 200n; political career, 36–38, 40–41, 82, 84; portrait, 35; reinterment, 118–19, 192–93n; secession & Confederacy, 7, 67–68, 117; Sherman, William T., 8–9, 10, 16, 27, 45–46, 108, 171n, 178n; slaves, 10, 12–13, 172n, 173n; University of North Carolina, president, 2, 3–4, 6, 26–27, 45–46, 67, 75–76, 106–08, 111, 145, 183n; UNC's debt to, 145, 152–53, 200–01n; UNC, resignation from, 76–77, 107–08, 111, 191n; Vance, Zebulon, 8, 131, 171–72n, 187n; White, Eleanor Hope, courtship & marriage to, 34, 36–38, 40–41, 176n, 177n. *See also* Chapel Hill; Raleigh, surrender of; University of North Carolina; *and individual children*

Swain, Eleanor (Ella). *See* Atkins, Eleanor (Ella) Hope Swain

Swain, Eleanor Louise (Lula), 85, 95, 96, 104, 110, 116, 119, 122, 126, 152, 194–96n, 200–01n

Swain, Eleanor White: Anne, death of 85–86, 186n; Atkins, Smith D., 25, 27, 41, 141, 148–50; background, 34, 184n, 189n, 208; Confederacy, loyalty to, 25, 27–28, 150, 177n; Ella, engagement & marriage of, 34, 41–42, 61, 66, 178–79n; estate, 151–53, 200–01n, 203n; move from Chapel Hill, 118–19, 192–93n; portrait, 39; reinterment of loved ones, 118–19, 192–93n; religion, 124, 178n, 193n; sisters, 26, 37, 40, 82, 84–85, 118, 132, 141, 192–93n, 199n; Swain, David L., courtship & marriage to, 34, 36–38, 40–41, 176n, 177n, 207; Swain, David L., papers of, 142–145, 151, 199n, 200–01n. *See also* Swain, David L.; White Hall; *and individual children and sisters*

Swain, George E., 36, 41, 181n, 187–89n, 194–95n, 207

Swain, "Infant Ella," 82, 86, 111, 118–19, 128–29

Swain, Margaret (Maggie) Louisa Steele, 95, 96, 104, 105, 115–16, 119, 122, 124–26, 127, 136, 194–96n. *See also* Swain, Eleanor Louise; Swain, Richard Caswell

Swain, Richard Caswell (Bunkey): birth, 82; Burt, Susan, 94, 124–27, 152, 194n; childhood, 10, 82, 129, 170n; education, 93–94, 187–89n; Ella, relationship with, 4–5, 93, 95, 96, 105, 136, 148; medical career, 93–96, 124, 189n; military career, 4–5, 94–95, 189n; photographs, 5, 125; post–traumatic stress, 94–95; Steele, Margaret, 95, 96, 104, 105. *See also* Swain, Eleanor Louise

Swain, Susan Burt, 94; reinterment, 118–19, 192–93n

Swain, Wilson, 10, 172n

Taylor, John Louis (Judge), 34, 36, 188n

Third Regiment Ulster County (N.Y.), 11

Thirty–ninth Regiment North Carolina Infantry, 94, 189n, 196n

Trumbull, Lyman (U.S. Sen.), 185n

Typographical Union, 166

Union army. *See* Atkins, Smith D.; Chapel Hill; Civil War

United States War Department, 29–30

University of North Carolina: Board of Trustees, 76–77, 107–08, 118, 142, 144–45, 152–53, 191n, 198n, 200–01n; charter, 107; Civil War, 1–4, 23, 26–28, 45–47, 106–07, 191n; closing, 107, 132; controversy, commencement, 76; controversy, Swain/Atkins courtship & marriage, 33, 45–46, 64–65, 67–68, 178n, 183n; enrollment, 6, 26, 131, 191n; financial difficulties, 6, 26–27, 67–68, 75–77, 106–08, 178n; Johnson, Andrew, 98, 106, 111–12; North Carolina Historical Society, 142–45; Reconstruction, 46, 64, 67–68, 75–77, 98, 106–08, 118, 142, 144–45, 183n, 191n; reopened, 131–32, 198n; Swain, David L., 23, 75–77, 106–08, 144–45, 150, 152–53, 191n, 194n, 200–01n; Swain, Eleanor White, 118–19, 142–45, 152–53; Union occupation of, 2–3, 10–13, 15–16, 23, 25–27, 169n, 178–79n. *See also* Chapel Hill

Vance, David, 131
Vance, Robert Brank, 36, 37
Vance, Zebulon (Gov.), 8–9, 62, 76, 131, 144, 171–72n. *See also* Graham, William; Raleigh, surrender; Swain, David L.
Vickers, James, 33

Walker, John, 64, 208
Walker, Sophronia White, 64, 82, 192n, 208
War of 1812, 11, 180n
Wheat, Selina, 25, 43, 85, 94, 124, 175n
Wheeler, Joseph (Maj. Gen.), 3–4, 7, 8–9, 10, 23, 27, 28–29, 170n
White, Ann (Nancy). *See* Barringer, Ann White
White, Anna Caswell, 37, 82, 184n, 208
White, Eleanor Hope. *See* Swain, Eleanor White
White, Elizabeth (Betsy). *See* Felton, Betsy White
White, Emma, 7, 26, 64, 82, 84–85, 118, 123, 132, 134, 141, 144, 184n, 186n, 192n, 198n, 199n, 208. *See also* Swain, Eleanor White; White Hall
White, Gartha, 37, 208
White Hall, 26, 37, 38, 40, 82, 118, 127, 132, 134, 141, 144, 177n, 186n, 192n, 199n
White, Susan, 42, 82, 84–85, 118, 141, 187–89n, 192n, 199n, 208. *See also* Swain, Eleanor White; White Hall
White, William, 34, 184n, 189n, 208
Wilder's Brigade, 56, 203n
Women: Civil War, in the, 6, 14, 23, 34, 63, 148, 150, 182n; confinement and pregnancy, 75; domesticity, 6, 43, 63, 89–93, 96–98, 119–20, 122–23, 132–36, 182n; education, 42–43, 178n
Women's Relief Corps, 162

Zion Episcopal Church, 75, 164

Acknowledgments

A project like *Undaunted Heart* is never the work of one person. It began as a story in the *Cary News* in 1994 when my editor, Jane Paige, indulged me by letting me write about Ella Swain Atkins's letters and her life with the Union general. Then came a variety of "Ella and Genl" research projects in graduate school and, finally, the Valentine's program in 2000 for the Chapel Hill Historical Society.

What a scene it was! Armed with a script, overhead transparencies, and photographs, I took the podium. When I saw Bill Powell, my UNC history professor, and North Carolina's Historian Emeritus, standing in the back of the room, I realized I might be in over my head. Was my research accurate? Did I know everything there was to know about Ella and Genl's story? I feared Professor Powell might throw his hands up and cry, "No! No! She's wrong!" Instead, he nodded approvingly as I spoke.

After that, I took my show on the road. My sisters Ellie Maynard—Ella's namesake—and Pattie Brooks helped gather family artifacts—jewelry, books, newspaper clippings, and photos; my friend Lisa Grable had the transparencies professionally copied, this being the pre-PowerPoint era.

At the urging of a dear colleague, the late Bettye Neff, I began writing *Undaunted Heart*. It took more than a decade. Along the way I discovered several cousins—Peg Isaac, Rod Speer, Eleanor Uhlinger, and Claire Hadley—who helped with research, and Liz Isaac, the spouse of a distant cousin, who was a wonderful editing partner, juggling work and family obligations while enthusiastically reading, making suggestions, and pressing me to keep writing.

I am indebted to my siblings, my dad, my nieces and nephews, and a large extended family and wealth of friends, who never let on if they did grow weary of hearing me talk about Ella and Genl. To my Wake Tech and N.C. Press Club colleagues, my long-time cheerleaders Laura Walters, Mejo Okon, and Gail Chesson, my college roomies, Libbie Farias and Gray Roth, and my mentor, Suzanne Tate, I offer thanks for their encouragement. To Professor Powell, who instilled in me an abiding love for North Carolina history, and to my editor and publisher, Elizabeth Woodman, who truly believed, I am forever grateful. I also want to thank Gita Schonfeld, Willis Whichard, Speed Hallman, and Doug Baker for their careful reading of the manuscript.

Finally to my daughter, Jen Brett, who loves Ella as much as I do; and to my husband, John, I am humbled by your never-say-never attitude.

Biography

After a twenty-five-year career as a newspaper reporter and editor, Suzy Barile teaches English and journalism at Wake Tech Community College in Raleigh, North Carolina. She is a graduate of the School of Journalism and Mass Communications at the University of North Carolina at Chapel Hill, and earned a master's degree from North Carolina State University.

An award-winning writer, Ms. Barile has contributed to the *North Carolina Encyclopedia* (edited by William S. Powell) and the *Book of American Traditions* (edited by Emyl Jenkins). Her articles have appeared in the *Cary News* (NC), *Triangle Business Journal* (NC), and the *News & Observer* (Raleigh), among other publications.

In 2001, she won the Paul Green Multi-Media Award from the North Carolina Society of Historians for her presentation of "The Governor's Daughter and the Yankee General." She is co-editor of "The Papers of Richard Caswell" for the North Carolina Office of Archives & History.

The great-great-granddaughter of Ella Swain Atkins and General Smith Dykins Atkins, Ms. Barile discovered in her mother's attic the letters Ella wrote to her own parents. These letters inspired her to research the much-storied romance of Ella and the general.

She lives in Cary, North Carolina.